Spiritual Leadership
for Church Officers

Spiritual Leadership for Church Officers

A Handbook

JOAN S. GRAY

Geneva Press
Louisville, Kentucky

First edition
Geneva Press
Louisville, Kentucky

Scripture quotations from the New Revised Standard Version of the Bible are copyright © 1989 by the Division of Christian Education of the National Council of the Churches of Christ in the U.S.A. and are used by permission.

Book design by Drew Stevens
Cover design by Mark Abrams

Cover art: The three Magi departing across the seas. From the Baptistery, Florence. Mosaics cover the entire cupola. They were begun in 1220 and completed a century later. The designs are by Florentine painters, among them Cimabue and the young Giotto. Baptistery, Florence, Italy. Photo Credit: Erich Lessing/Art Resource, NY.

Library of Congress Cataloging-in-Publication Data

Gray, Joan S.
  Spiritual leadership for church officers : a handbook / Joan S. Gray.
      p. cm.
  Includes bibliographical references and index.
  ISBN 978-0-664-50305-5 (alk. paper)
  1. Elders (Church officers)   2. Pastoral theology.   3. Christian leadership.   I. Title.
  BV680.G73 2009
  253—dc22

2009001916

PRINTED IN THE UNITED STATES OF AMERICA

♾ The paper used in this publication meets the minimum requirements of the American National Standard for Information Sciences—Permanence of Paper for Printed Library Materials, ANSI Z39.48-1992.

Geneva Press advocates the responsible use of our natural resources. The text paper of this book is made from at least 30% postconsumer waste.

This book is dedicated to my husband, Bill Gray,
ruling elder of the PC(USA)
and my strong support through thirty years of ministry

Contents

Introduction

Read the book of Acts and you will enter a world of churches without clergy, at least without clergy as we know that profession today. The ancient church was basically lay-led. In each city they visited, roving evangelists like Paul, Barnabas, and Apollos gathered small groups of believers. These groups met in homes and for a time were taught and formed by the ministry of the evangelist. However, evangelists were not long-term pastors; they were rolling stones always going on to the next place to spread the word. Eventually the founder moved on and left the fledgling church in the hands of its members, who selected their own leaders from among themselves.

Today most Presbyterian churches have ministers of the Word and Sacrament serving them in some pastoral capacity. Yet elders, and deacons if present, are still the backbone of any Presbyterian church, and few churches rise far above the level of their lay leadership. I say this not to devalue the role and work of the pastor or pastors in a congregation, but because even the most dynamic and gifted pastor is hamstrung if the congregation's lay leaders are lethargic, conflicted, or spiritually anemic. Churches come alive in new ways when clergy and laity both catch a vision for mission and are empowered by the Holy Spirit. Expecting spiritual combustion to happen only through the efforts of the clergy is like expecting a match to set fire to a pile of sodden logs. Depending on how wet the logs are, even a blowtorch might not do the job! Churches face staggering challenges and opportunities. In such a time, nothing is more important than leadership—specifically, the quality of the spiritual leadership of the church's officers.

Even so, the care and feeding of officers is a low priority in many churches. Officer training is often perfunctory and tends toward a review of the high points of the *Book of Order*. Officer retreats frequently focus on church business rather than on the nurture of the spirit. Although officers are the heavy lifters of the church, they are generally expected to make it on their own, using whatever they can glean from worship and church school to sustain them in their work. Presbyterian churches do our elders a great disservice when we neglect their spiritual growth in this way.

To be fair, some officers feel they don't need any special training or nurture; perhaps they've served on the board of the Girl Scouts or the United Way. They know what an officer is and how a board is supposed to operate. The session or board of deacons may seem no different to them than the board of any nonprofit corporation. Others feel that the pastor should be the spiritual leader of the church, with everyone else doing whatever he or she says. The idea that the officers themselves might be called to be spiritual leaders makes them nervous. Still others don't want to waste their time on things that are not directly related to church business; they are busy people, and their time is too precious to waste on nonproductive activities. "We're here to get a job done!" is their theme song, and the sooner it gets done and they can go home the better.

Given all of the above, it is little wonder that many church officers come to the end of their term deeply weary, spiritually drained, and swearing that they will never do it again. Members of a church I served years ago talked about people who had once been very active, but I had never met them. I asked someone where these people were. "Oh, those are our past clerks of session. It seems that after someone serves as clerk for a couple of years, he or she is so burned out they leave the church. Sometimes they come back after a while, sometimes they don't." I remember thinking, *No wonder this church has such trouble finding people who are willing to serve as officers!*

People accept the call to be leaders in the church for a wide variety of reasons. At least some of them do so because they hope to deepen their faith and grow as Christians. I learned this at a business-as-usual Monday night session meeting some years ago. The elders were trying hard to concentrate, although many were weary after a long workday. The topic of the annual session retreat was next on the agenda. When I finished my report on retreat plans and asked for comments, John, the chairman of the building and grounds committee, said, "One of the reasons I became an elder was I thought it would bring me closer to God, but the opposite has happened." For a long moment no one moved or spoke. Then others began to share similar feelings and longings. That night I became aware that many elders are looking for something more than business as usual from their term of service. They are looking for a deepened relationship with God.

If strong churches need strong officers, then we should be doing everything in our power to help elders and deacons grow in their relationship to God. Unfortunately they are most often left to their own devices, to sink or swim as best they can. This book is written for officers who want to be effective spiritual leaders and want to grow closer to God as they serve the church.

To that end, chapter 1 introduces spiritual leadership and the role of elders and deacons as spiritual leaders in Presbyterian churches. Chapter 2 deals with the authority needed to lead and where it comes from. The third chapter employs the metaphor of a rowboat and a sailboat to address leading and living with the church in a manner that is deeply empowered by the Holy Spirit. Chapters 4 and 5 continue this theme by setting forth attitudes, practices, and skills that make for effective leadership in a Spirit-powered church. Chapter 6 lays out a variety of leadership styles for working with people and helps leaders understand when each might be most appropriate. The nature of the church as both a human and divine institution is the subject of chapter 7, drawing out some implications for leadership of this unique nature. Chapter 8 provides resources for dealing with interpersonal relationships in the church using some principles of family systems theory. Understanding spiritual discernment and how it shapes the life of a leader and his or her church is addressed in chapter 9. Chapter 10 considers how churches can create a positive atmosphere for the spiritual leadership of elders and deacons and also explores what the officers themselves can do to grow and become more effective in their work.

This book is written out of a deep respect and affection for church officers. Few things have given me more joy than working with many wonderful, committed elders and deacons throughout thirty years of ministry. Through thick and thin, knowing that I was not alone but part of a team of Christians seeking God's will has made all the difference. I also write out of a conviction that the spiritual health of church officers is crucial to the church's welfare.

Pastors cannot and should not bear the burden of leadership alone. My prayer is that pastors and officers together would use this book to empower the spiritual leadership of the laity, so we all might find that the yoke of serving Christ's church is eased and the burden is made light.

1

Elders and Deacons Are Spiritual Leaders

Elders and deacons are, with pastors, the spiritual leaders of Presbyterian Church (U.S.A.) congregations. To begin to understand what their leadership is about, we must first understand what church membership means. According to the *Book of Order*, "One becomes an active member of the church through faith in Jesus Christ as Savior and acceptance of his Lordship in all of life" (G-5.0101a). The word "faith" as it is used here does not mean simply an intellectual belief in God. Rather, "Faith is a personal and immediate relationship to God."[1] Church membership is rooted in this kind of human-divine bond made possible for us by Jesus Christ and brought about in us by the Holy Spirit. The relationship then bears the fruit of ministry.

Many Christians think of ministry as something the clergy do. Not so, according to the Bible. The Holy Spirit gives each Christian a spiritual gift or gifts to be used "for the common good" (1 Cor. 12:7). God raises up among the Christians in a congregation the gifts needed to carry on ministry in that place. Among the many gifts mentioned in Scripture are hospitality, generosity, teaching, preaching, administration, and healing. However, the Spirit is not limited to any particular list of gifts and is constantly at work in the congregation and beyond it, drawing and cultivating the particular gifts needed for mission and ministry there.

For example, a wonderful ministry is to call the children and teens of the congregation by name and make them feel valued. So, too, is

1

greeting visitors and new members. Dealing with money is an important ministry in every church week in and week out, and being able to do it gracefully is a gift. I have known people who had never taught or worked with children but who volunteered to teach because teachers were needed. They found that as they got into the work, they were given what they needed to do it—and teaching became a joy! This is the Spirit at work empowering the ministry of ordinary church members. "Every member a minister" is not just a slogan. It states a biblical truth that has shaped the Presbyterian Church from its earliest days.

Out of this understanding of ministry as a part of church membership comes the practice of electing and ordaining officers—pastors, elders, and deacons—to carry out particular tasks in the life of the church. Elders are set apart, along with pastors, to lead and govern the church. Deacons are set apart for ministries of compassion and service. Pastors, of course, are also set apart for the ministry of Word and Sacrament. The *Book of Order* is quick to point out, however, "The existence of these offices in no way diminishes the importance of the commitment of all members to the total ministry of the church. These ordained officers differ from other members in function only" (G-6.0102).

Just as church membership grows out of a relationship with Jesus Christ, so ministry in the church, especially ordained ministry (elders, deacons, and ministers of Word and Sacrament) is to be carried out in a way that reflects his character. John's Gospel tells us that shortly before Jesus went to the cross, he gathered his disciples together for a meal. During the meal, Jesus rose from the table and, taking a basin and towel, began to wash and dry his disciples' feet. In that day, household slaves usually did this task. When he finished, Jesus said to them, "If I, your Lord and Teacher, have washed your feet, you also ought to wash one another's feet. For I have set you an example, that you also should do as I have done to you" (John 13:14–15). The ministry of church officers, along with that of all Christians, is to be carried out in imitation of Christ, who showed his love by serving.

WHAT IS A SPIRITUAL LEADER?

For Christians the word "spiritual" will always be somehow connected with the Holy Spirit. Before Jesus went to the cross, he promised his disciples an "Advocate, the Holy Spirit, whom the Father will send in my name" (John 14:26). The Advocate would function to teach the disciples the truth about Jesus and also to empower them to follow him in his ministry. The Spirit would help them love one another as Jesus commanded. All this and more came from the gift of the Holy Spirit after Jesus' earthly presence was withdrawn from the first believers.

The Spirit also works to turn believers into people of the Spirit, making their character and actions reflect those of Christ. This new way of being is a gift of God, not anything an individual can earn or create. The apostle Paul says to the Ephesians, "You were dead through the trespasses and sins in which you once lived" (Eph. 2:1–2). However, through the love of God, the redeeming work of Jesus on the cross, and the power of the Holy Spirit, they were brought out of death into freedom and abundant life. People who live by the Spirit will show the fruit of the Spirit— that is, they will demonstrate in their daily lives "love, joy, peace, patience, kindness, generosity, faithfulness, gentleness, and self-control" (Gal. 5:22–23). These virtues are not self-created, but rather are the results of a relationship with the living Christ.

What do I mean by "spiritual leader"? Let's start with the word "spiritual." A spiritual leader is one whose way of life is centered in a relationship to the God revealed in Jesus Christ and empowered by the Holy Spirit. Notice that spirituality is about a way of life. As such, it pertains to everything we do, all the time. It is not something we turn on when we go to church and turn off when we go out into the world. Spirituality is not a separate piece of life that we plug in when we have the time or feel like it.

True Christian spirituality is the warp and woof of the believer's daily existence. It includes practices and attitudes that not only encourage faith in the believer but also make a difference in the world. True Spirituality is just as at home in the workplace as it is in the sanctuary. It comes into play not only when we read the Bible, but also when we read the newspaper. Spirituality is not only about religion but has something to say about how we spend our money, raise our children, run our businesses, and cast our vote. People of the Spirit bear the fruit of the Spirit at church certainly, but also in every other area of life as well.

The other important word here is "leader." In the most general sense, a leader exercises authority or influence to motivate other people to follow her or him. Leadership implies movement and change. People who have no desire to go anywhere usually do not need a leader; they will be most happy with someone who functions as a guardian or custodian. Leaders have a vision of something that is not yet accomplished. They are heading for a destination and want to take others with them. They see things that could be and are drawn to put their energies into galvanizing others in order to make those visions realities.

As I use the term in this book, a spiritual leader leads others to seek and do God's will. Sometimes people take up this leadership eagerly. Others become spiritual leaders only with reluctance. Moses is perhaps the most famous example of a reluctant spiritual leader. He was not looking for a new occupation when he met God at the burning bush. He argued with God about his credentials and his competence for the job. At first glance it might seem that Moses was not qualified to be a spiritual leader. After all, years earlier when he saw an Egyptian beating one of his fellow Hebrews, "He looked this way and that, and seeing no one he killed the Egyptian and hid him in the sand" (Exod. 2:12). Yet God insisted that Moses was the one to lead the Hebrew people toward the goal of living in the promised land, and the third chapter of Exodus tells how at the burning bush, he was both called to be a spiritual leader and given the authority necessary for leadership. Like Moses, some officers may feel unworthy and unqualified for their call, but as the old saying goes: God does not call the qualified; God qualifies the called.

ELDERS: LEADERS IN GOVERNANCE

If you are a Presbyterian elder, you belong to a group that is almost without parallel in Christianity. Talk with your friends who are Methodist, Baptist, or Catholic, and you will find that nothing in their churches resembles this distinctive office. In churches with a congregational style of church government, as Baptists have, the power to make decisions governing the life of the congregation is exercised by the congregation itself. In principle this system is pure democracy in action. Each member has a vote, and the majority rules. Persons elected to serve as officers carry out the congregation's decisions and may propose matters to the congregation for action, but the final decision is made in the congregational meeting.

At the other end of the spectrum, in churches with episcopal polity, the power to govern is by and large exercised through varying ranks of clergy. Laity may serve as advisers or act in committees to propose certain courses of action, but bishops or other clergy generally make final decisions on many matters central to the life of the congregation.

In contrast, Presbyterian congregations elect elders who join with pastors in groups that oversee the congregation's life and make policy decisions: "Together with ministers of the Word and Sacrament, [elders] exercise leadership, government, and discipline and have responsibilities for the life of a particular church as well as the church at large" (G-6.0302). One of the unique aspects of this system is that when elders and clergy sit in governing bodies together, their power is equal: each has one vote, and all votes are equal. The *Book of Order* requires that a certain number of elders, in addition to clergy, must be present in order for any session, presbytery, synod, or General Assembly meeting to transact business legally. Elders are also eligible to hold all the elected offices of the church, including that of Moderator of the General Assembly.

Elders are so central to Presbyterian polity that without them, no method of church government could dare to call itself "Presbyterian." This unique office has its roots deep in history. The very word "presbyterian" is derived from the Greek word *presbyteros*, meaning "old" or "elder." The ancient world was very familiar with the rule of elders who were responsible for overseeing the welfare of their communities. Long before the nation of Israel came into existence, we read about elders in Scripture (see Gen. 50:7; Num. 22:4, 7; Josh. 9:11).

The *Book of Order* begins its description of the office of elder by telling us that "as there were in Old Testament times elders for the government of the people, so the New Testament Church provided persons with particular gifts to share in governing and ministry" (G-6.0301). In organizing itself, the early church was influenced by a familiar institution: the Jewish synagogue, which is not surprising, since all the earliest believers were Jews.

The synagogue came on the scene in the sixth century BC, around the time the Israelites were taken into exile in Babylon. It functioned both as a place of worship and a center for community life. Various members of the synagogue functioning together were often responsible for both the spiritual and temporal business of the faith community in that place. Their duties included seeing that worship services were carried out in a decent and orderly fashion, inviting persons in the congregation to lead the congregation in worship, handling the business matters of the community, encouraging people to keep the law, teaching children, keeping records, and exercising discipline if necessary. Some evidence exists that in later Judaism women may have served as officials of the synagogue.[2]

While it is difficult to make ironclad deductions about early church leadership from the New Testament writings, it can be argued that along with apostles, prophets, and evangelists, elders held a prominent role in those first Christian communities. Elders in the earliest days were often the men and women in whose homes the small groups of believers met. Lydia is an example of one such leader (Acts 16:11–40). These first elders were gifted by the Holy Spirit for leadership and administration. Their focus was the overall health and welfare of the local congregation:

> It was the elders at Jerusalem who received the gift for famine relief from the church at Antioch (Acts 11:30), and who helped to decide the basis on which Gentiles should be received into the church (Acts 15:2, 4, 6, 22–23; 16:4). Paul and Barnabas appointed elders for each of the churches they established on their first missionary trip (Acts 14:32). . . . Paul requests a special gathering with the elders of the church at Ephesus on his way back to Jerusalem (Acts 20:17). . . . James calls for the involvement of the elders in prayers for the sick (James 5:14).[3]

These elders, like their ancient Jewish counterparts, worked as a group to ensure that the community of faith was healthy. In addition to concern for the public witness of the church, elders interested themselves in the "inner health [of the church], in the climate or environment in which the members lived."[4] These earliest Christian elders worked to create a communal environment where the gospel flourished and was shared with others as a powerful source of new life. It takes little imagination to believe that, on a human level, the church owes its continued existence to the ministry of those early elders. They were the ones who preserved the teachings of the faith through hard times and encouraged the people to stand strong in times of persecution.

Over the centuries, as the church went from being a persecuted sect to the established religion of the Roman Empire, the clergy became more prominent and powerful, and the ministry of elders seemed to die out. Much scholarly ink has been spilled discussing why this happened, but the fact remains that priests and bishops increasingly carried out the preaching, teaching, and administration of the congregations. Since in many communities only the clergy could read, even the Scripture itself was only available to people through the priest. Much of the unordained Christians' evangelical zeal and burning desire to serve Christ in these centuries was channeled into monastic life, for in the parish churches, the clergy generally ruled.

Then came the movement known as the Reformation. John Calvin, the father of the Presbyterian or Reformed movement, created a system in Geneva, Switzerland, in the sixteenth century where city and church were governed as one. For help in structuring and organizing this governmental system, Calvin looked to the accounts of the second-century church in the pastoral epistles and came up with a structure consisting of four offices: pastor, doctor or teacher, ruling elder, and deacon, each with its own responsibilities. Pastors preached, administered sacraments, and performed funerals, baptisms, and other such rites. Those who held the office of teacher, also called doctor, were largely responsible for the education of children as well as adults. Ruling elders had the task of maintaining order and discipline in the community. Deacons cared for the poor, including administering monies given to charity.

Calvin's ruling elders were nonclergy "representing various parishes of the city and related to both the church and civic government. They took an oath similar to that prescribed for the ministers. They met once each week with the pastors in a body known as the consistory to hear complaints against immoralities, or indecent language, or doctrinal errors, and any other matters that might corrupt the purity of the church and bring reproach to its good name."[5] John Calvin largely laid the foundation on which is built the system that we have today: clergy and lay leaders having equal power but different duties, meeting together to see to the spiritual welfare and order of the body of Christ.

DEACONS: LEADERS IN SERVICE

The title "deacon" comes from a Greek word meaning servant; benevolent service, rather than governance, has generally been the function of deacons through the centuries. One reason the early church spread so quickly is that its members showed an extraordinary degree of care for those who were orphaned, widowed, poor, sick, or friendless. As we see in Acts 4:34–35, "There was not a needy person among them, for as many as owned lands or houses sold them and brought the proceeds of what was sold. They laid it at the apostles' feet, and it was distributed to each as any had need."

Ironically, however, this very generosity occasioned the first recorded conflict in the church. Acts 6 tells how the believers who were of Greek background felt that the Greek widows were being neglected while the Hebrew widows received plenty in the daily distribution of food. This disagreement was the last straw for the apostles, whose energies were so drained by administrative tasks relating to the church's charities that the evangelistic mission was suffering.

From this situation in the early church the officer of deacon was born. The first deacons were "seven men of good standing, full of the Spirit and of wisdom" (Acts 6:3). Their work was a blessing to the church, and the writer of Acts tells us that after the deacons were appointed, "The word of God continued to spread; the number of the disciples increased greatly in Jerusalem, and a great many of the priests became obedient to the faith" (Acts 6:7). After reading this story in Scripture, Calvin concluded, "Here, then, is the kind of deacons the apostolic church had, and which we, after their example, should have."[6]

The crucial importance of the office of deacon grows out of the obligation of the church to care for those in need. This obligation is not an optional activity, but rather one of the ways that disciples live out their relationship to their Lord. As such, caring for the poor must always be a core value for the church and part of its ministry in every place and time. Matthew's Gospel goes so far as to say that Christians will be judged for all eternity on the basis of how we have treated the hungry, the thirsty, strangers, the sick, those without clothing, and those in prison. Jesus identifies so completely with these people that to do something, or not to do it, for one of them is the same as doing it or not doing it for him (see Matt. 25:31–46).

The work of ministering to those in need is so crucial to the spiritual health and mission of the church that it cannot be left up to individual believers. Writing on the subject of deacons in 1879, Presbyterian minister James B. Ramsey argued that "the care of the poor, relieving their wants and soothing their sorrows, and encouraging their crushed spirits, is, therefore, a duty entwined in the very nature of Christian life—springing naturally and necessarily out of the believer's union with Christ."[7] The church as a whole must take responsibility for this work as an ongoing part of its mission, and as in Bible times, delegating this work to deacons is the most efficient approach.

Given this history, that the original caring, mission-focused calling of deacons often changed into managing the business affairs of the congregation is puzzling. Often when this shift occurred, conflicts and power struggles developed between the board of deacons and the session. Since all decisions made by the deacons had to be approved and could be overturned by the session, the two bodies often seemed to be duplicating each other's work. In time the *Book of Order* was amended to allow congregations to vote to dispense with the office of deacon altogether, and all the duties that had been carried out by deacons became responsibilities of the elders.

The last twenty years have seen a movement in the church to revive the office of deacon and restore it to its true biblical function. As a result, the *Book of Order* notes that, first and foremost, "the office of deacon as set forth in Scripture is one of sympathy, witness, and service after the example of Jesus Christ. . . . It is the duty of deacons, first of all, to minister to those who are in need, to the sick, to the friendless, and to any who may be in distress both within and beyond the community of faith" (G-6.0401, 0402).

Here we have the heart of the deacons' calling. They are to lead the church in fulfilling the command of Christ to serve the poor and friendless. Deacons are charged with keeping this work before the church and making sure that the resources are in place to carry it out. They may do this while organized as a board of deacons or they may work as individuals. However they are organized, their leadership in the church's ministry to those in need is absolutely essential to the church's spiritual health.

QUESTIONS FOR THOUGHT AND DISCUSSION

1. Think about someone you have known whom you would call an effective spiritual leader. What were the characteristics, habits, or practices that made that person effective?
2. Faith in God involves having a relationship with God. How would you describe your relationship with God?
3. What do you think your spiritual gifts are? How have you used them to strengthen your church? How have you used them outside the church?
4. When you hear the word "spirituality," what comes to your mind?
5. What is your reaction to this statement? "The primary work of a Presbyterian session is to lead a congregation to seek and do God's will."

2

Your Authority to Lead

On the playground, one child tells another to do something. The child receiving the order replies indignantly, "You are not the boss of me!" What's the issue here? Authority. A teacher who is not much older than the high school students in his classroom may have trouble exercising effective discipline. Lack of authority is the root of the problem. A mother wears a T-shirt proclaiming, "Because I'm the mom, that's why!" She is making a statement about authority. When employees challenged Henry Ford about business matters, from time to time he would assert his authority by saying, "We'll do it that way because it's my name on the building."[1] The session votes relating to a particular matter, but before the ink dries on the minutes of the meeting, certain church members are already at work to undermine what has been done. The session's authority is being challenged.

Authority and leadership are intertwined. Authority is what enables leaders to motivate followers to move together toward a goal. A leader without followers is a committee of one, so grasping where authority comes from and how it is granted by those whom you would lead is important. Authority has a number of sources. First, in the church the ultimate source of a person's spiritual authority is that person's call from God to serve. "It belongs to Christ alone to rule, to teach, to call, and to use the Church as he wills, *exercising his authority by the ministry of women and men for the establishment and extension of his Kingdom*" (G-1.0100b, emphasis added). At the deepest level, all authority exercised in the church belongs to Jesus Christ; Christ delegates spiritual authority to those called to lead.

Presbyterians take very seriously this call of God to service. In the Presbyterian Church the very fact that you have been elected, ordained, and installed gives you a basic authority to lead. The situation is similar to that of elected government officials; they have authority to do their job by means of their election. They are empowered to function in this way throughout their term of office unless impeached or otherwise lawfully removed.

Further, the authority to lead is also granted to church officers through the traditions of our church, particularly Scripture and our Presbyterian theology. As we have seen, Calvin based the offices of deacon and elder on the foundation of Holy Scripture. The Presbyterian Church does not claim that ours is the only form of church government that is faithful to Scripture; nor do we judge or condemn other churches for doing things differently. However, we continue to point to Scripture as our basis for the offices of elder and deacon. Since the Bible and our tradition support government by elders and service by deacons, most Presbyterians automatically grant these officers a certain amount of authority.

The tradition and history of each particular congregation around its leadership also function to give or take away authority. If past leaders earned the respect, trust, and confidence of the parishioners and thus were granted great authority as leaders, their successors may find it easy to exercise leadership in that congregation.[2] However, if there has been a tradition of incompetence, bad judgment, dishonesty, or conflict among elders or deacons, members will be less responsive to their current officers. In these situations, confidence must be restored before anyone can lead.

Finally, authority is granted to officers by the constitution of the Presbyterian Church. The *Book of Order* gives elders certain rights and responsibilities as spiritual leaders. Meeting as a session, they are responsible for overseeing the entire life and mission of the congregation and all the groups in the church. Among other things, the form of government gives sessions authority to set the church budget, decide what types of activities can be held in the church buildings, approve or disapprove of teachers and activities in the church's programs, receive new members, hire and fire nonclergy employees of the church, set the time and place of worship, and elect the church's commissioners to the presbytery. The session does not need to ask anyone's permission to do these things; the *Book of Order* authorizes the session to lead in these areas. Deacons likewise are authorized by our polity to carry out the church's benevolent ministry under the oversight of the session.

All these sources of authority are granted by virtue of office because of our Presbyterian constitution, history, and traditions. However, if they are the sole sources of your authority, your leadership will probably not be highly effective. To mobilize followers and motivate them to move toward mutually desired goals, leaders must also exercise authority that is evoked personally by the way they live their lives and go about their work in the church.

This deeper kind of authority flows from the character and actions of the individual leader and the collected leadership. It must be inspired in and granted by those who are followers. People give leaders authority based on those leaders' characteristics and actions. Qualities such as emotional maturity, honesty, personal achievement, life experience, the ability to speak well, and a compassionate nature can inspire confidence in followers so that they give authority to leaders. These personal characteristics are often the unspoken, almost unconscious parts of the leadership equation and are often not mentioned in discussions about a person's qualifications to serve.

One of the characteristics people look for in church leaders before granting such authority is a serious commitment to the congregation. Has she been around for a good while? Has he shown commitment by working regularly in the church? Has she been willing to take on difficult jobs? Does he seem to be only a fair-weather church member, or will he still be there when problems and conflicts come? The willingness to work through trouble is often a test of commitment; people do not want leaders who are going to jump ship when the going gets rough. Members are more willing to follow those in whom they sense a real commitment to the welfare of the church over the long term.

Another factor in gaining the trust of a congregation is the degree to which people feel their leader sets the larger interests of that congregation ahead of his or her own. This approach requires rising above the desire for personal good in order to do what is best for the whole, avoiding actions that may make you feel good but which may stir up trouble in the church, and setting aside personal preferences when something else will work better for the whole group. When people feel their leaders are acting for the congregation's good instead of only their own, the congregation is much more willing to grant leaders authority.

Closely related to this concept is that people look for good intentions in their leaders. A congregation will not trust someone whom they believe is trying to undermine the good of the church. I remember one church member who loved to visit new and prospective members of the church. The problem was that wherever he went, he spread complaints and discontent. He complained about the pastor, he spread gossip about other members, he harped on everything that was wrong and hardly ever mentioned what was right in the church. Whether he realized it or not, he was undermining the pastor and clouding the good name of the church; because both were very important to the congregation, no one trusted him, and he was never elected to office in that church.

The personal trait of trustworthiness is another crucial source of authority for leaders. Leadership often involves asking people to move out of their comfort zone and take a risk in order to move toward a goal, and people are not willing to risk much or go very far with leaders they cannot trust. Trust must be earned, which is accomplished by such basic behavior as telling the truth, even when no one wants to hear it. Nothing discourages people from granting trust more than lying. Even small lies, when found out, do serious damage to trust.

Another source of authority for leaders is competence. Do people have a sense that you know what you are doing? Are you able to answer questions knowledgeably? Are you in touch with what is going on in the church and able to communicate that to others? Can you chair a meeting so that people both enjoy themselves and do their jobs efficiently? Can you handle people with grace and good humor? Do you know enough of the Bible, theology, and the *Book of Order* to function well? Do you make wise decisions that stand the test of time? Do people see the church flourishing and moving forward in mission under your leadership? Do you do your homework before meetings? All of these things help people decide whether or not a leader is competent.

Even so, I feel that competence is the least important source of authority for a leader. If people feel their leaders are trustworthy, of godly character, and willing to rise above self-interest, and have good intentions, they will forgive a certain amount of ineptitude. After all, incompetence can often be remedied by training; changing one's nature is much harder. The most powerful streams of authority are those that flow out of a person's character and the congregation's perception of her or his relationship with God.

Does this officer, as the saying goes, walk the walk as well as talk the talk? Do people sense that faith is real for this elder or deacon—not just something to which she gives lip service, but a deep and vital part of her life? Scripture tells us that when Moses came down from the mountaintop after spending time with God, the skin of his face was shining (Exod. 34:29–35). Being with God had rubbed off on him. So it will be with us when we spend time in God's company on a regular basis and commune with God throughout the day.

The important thing here is not so much how you feel about your spirituality, but how the congregation perceives it. Moses did not know his face was shining, but the people could see it and they knew he had been with God. Some of the most spiritual people I know would be horrified to hear that others think of them as saints. They know their own hearts too well; in the words of the psalmist, their sins are ever before them. Their self-deprecation can be a function of an overactive conscience, but it may also be a godly humility born of self-knowledge. When a log is put on the fire and the heat begins to penetrate, the bugs that have lived inside that log begin to come out. To look at the log from the outside, you would never know there were bugs in it. Similarly, when the fire of the Spirit begins to burn inside believers, they become increasingly aware of their own sins and imperfections, of how far short they fall from loving God with their whole heart and loving their neighbors as themselves. Yet these folks are deeply dedicated to God and devoted to seeking God's will in all of life. Most Christians respect this kind of humility and commitment and often give these people authority to lead, either formally or informally.

Just being duly called, elected, ordained, and installed gives you a basic authority to function as an officer in a Presbyterian congregation. However, the ability to motivate people to follow your leadership, especially when the path is challenging and requires sacrifice, requires a deeper authority, which is granted or not as people see how you conduct yourself over time and whether or not you practice the faith you proclaim. No one expects you to be perfect, but the genuineness of an authentic relationship with God and a true desire to serve always shine through and inspire confidence.

QUESTIONS FOR THOUGHT AND DISCUSSION

1. Think back to your early experiences in a congregation. Who were the people you remember who exercised authority? What was the source of their authority?

2. Reflect on the ways officers are nominated, elected, and trained in your congregation. What about these processes tends to build up the authority of officers, or take it away?
3. What are the characteristics in a leader that tend to evoke trust or mistrust?
4. Is leadership in the church inherently different from leadership in business or civic settings? If so, why?

3

Rowboat or Sailboat?

Go back in your imagination to the Last Supper, the final meeting Jesus had with all his disciples before he was betrayed, tried, and crucified. Look around at the group gathered that night in the upper room. There is Judas, who will betray Jesus. There is Philip, who after several years with Jesus still doesn't understand who he is. James and John are jockeying for the best seats at the table. Thomas, who will refuse to believe the resurrection news, is there with Peter, who before the night is over will deny Jesus three times. The Gospels tell us that when the soldiers arrested Jesus, all the disciples ran away.

During that final meal together, Jesus looked at this confused, anxiety-ridden group and said an amazing thing: "The one who believes in me will also do the works that I do and, in fact, will do greater works than these, because I am going to the Father" (John 14:12). Surely Jesus was joking. How could he possibly look at Peter, Thomas, and the rest and suggest that they could ever do greater things than he had done? Jesus' promise is clear, but the human weakness and inability of those men sitting around that table is even clearer. The disciples simply did not have what Jesus had.

Even after the resurrection, the disciples misunderstood what Jesus was doing and their own part in it. Luke tells us that on the day Jesus ascended into heaven, they asked him, "Lord, is this the time when you will restore the kingdom to Israel?" (Acts 1:6). They are asking Jesus for insider information so they can be ready for the coming action. They are eager to jump into what they are absolutely sure is God's agenda. In spite of the unpleasantness of the cross, Jesus had returned triumphant. They are ready to see him take his rightful place as Messiah with the Romans defeated and Israel a proud, sovereign nation once more. Jesus quickly tells them that what they are so interested in knowing is none of their business. In so many words, Jesus says to the disciples, "You are not ready yet. You don't have what you need to put this thing together and make it work. You don't really even understand what I am doing. Something is missing, and until you receive what I will send you, you can do nothing." His command to go back to Jerusalem and wait must have felt like cold water thrown in their faces.

THE CHURCH IS LAUNCHED

Many of our churches today are decorated with symbols that come out of the early days of Christianity. The cross is the most familiar symbol, pointing to Jesus' saving death. An eye is a symbol for God. A symbol for the church that comes from these early days is a boat. In Jesus' time, there were two ways to power a boat on open water. One way was to use muscles, most commonly by rowing. The other way was to harness the power of the wind. A significant point is that when early Christians used a boat as a symbol for the church, it was never a rowboat; it was always a sailboat. The reason is that on the day of Pentecost, with "a sound like a rushing wind," Jesus' promise of power became a reality. In receiving the Holy Spirit that day, the believers found what they had been missing.

Jesus' promise of "power from on high" is not something new for God's people. On Pentecost, Peter quotes Joel's Hebrew Bible prophecy of a day when "your sons and your daughters shall prophesy." Jesus himself was full of the Holy Spirit and of God's power. Before this Pentecost experience, however, the Holy Spirit had generally been sent by God upon certain people as special equipment to accomplish certain things: prophecy, miracles, victory in battle, and so on. Now the Holy Spirit was poured out upon the whole community of believers, enabling them to fulfill Jesus' promise to do what he did and even greater things.

The book of Acts tells the story of how from the day of Pentecost onward, the Holy Spirit worked within the first believers to help them understand the true meaning of Jesus' life, teachings, death, and resurrection. The Spirit drew together a diverse group of men and women into a strong, unified community. The Spirit empowered the preaching of the believers and accompanied it with signs and wonders pointing to God's gracious salvation, guiding and leading the believers in discerning God's will and giving them courage when they ran afoul of political and religious authorities. The Spirit of God did for them what they could not do themselves, and before long blew them out of Jerusalem to change the world forever.

The early believers used a sailboat to symbolize the church because the idea of being powered by the Holy Spirit of God, as the wind moves a boat, was at the heart of their experience of being church. From the beginning the church was intended to be a God-powered movement. On Pentecost, the believers found what they had been missing, the gift of spiritual resources to participate with Jesus in his transformation of the world. As they felt the wind of the Spirit begin to blow around them that day, they raised their sails and began the process of learning how to become sailors. The book of Acts is the story of how God used their obedient faithfulness to do amazing things.

ARE YOU A ROWBOAT OR SAILBOAT CHURCH?

The leaders of a church, its pastors and officers, make the crucial choices about how that congregation is going to go forward. In effect, they decide whether the church will operate like a rowboat or a sailboat. The key difference between these two ways of being church is often not apparent on the surface. Both kinds of churches may be active and growing; both may struggle and even die. Both may engage in significant mission projects. Whether a church is liberal, conservative, or middle-of-the-road is no indication of whether it is a sailboat or a rowboat. Both types of church can be found in urban, suburban, and rural areas. The basic difference between them has nothing to do with the circumstances of a congregation; rather, the difference is in the attitude of the leadership and members.

The bedrock reality of life in the rowboat church is that God has given the church a basic agenda (for example, to make the world a better place, save souls, help the poor, spread Christian truth, etc.) and then left it up to the church to get on with it. The dominant attitude in this congregation is either "*We* can do this" or "*We* can't do this." The church's progress depends on circumstances like the amount of money in the bank, the number of volunteers available, the charisma and skill of its leaders, and the demographics of its community. Leaders in a rowboat church spend a large portion of their time focusing on such issues, and the key question becomes, "What can we do with what we have?" The presence or absence of resources largely determines what can be done. When these things are favorable, rowboat churches may go fast and far. But success depends on the resources it has in hand, the circumstances around them, and how hard its people are willing to row to get the job done.

In contrast, the dominant attitude in a sailboat church is that "God can do more than we can ask or imagine." Its leaders know that what they have or lack in the way of human and material resources is not the decisive factor in what they can accomplish as a church. Rather, they look on church as a continuing adventure with a God who leads and empowers them to do more than they could ever have dreamed. This adventure involves believers in an intimate relationship with the triune God who guides their life as a church.

Leaders of a sailboat church do not begin their planning by assuming they know God's agenda and adding up the resources they have to accomplish it. Rather the key question is, "What is God leading us to be and do now in the place where we find ourselves?" They are willing to spend considerable time and energy on discerning where God is moving and where God is inviting them to invest themselves in God's work. They take this approach because they believe that the God who calls is also the God who provides, and that if they are invested in doing what God wants the church to do, God will provide the resources.

BETWEEN NOTHING AND EVERYTHING

People who are committed to move forward with God in a sailboat church live between two realities. The first of these we hear from Jesus on the occasion of his last gathering with his disciples: "Apart from me you can do nothing" (John 15:5). "Nothing" is a very harsh word. It must have been hard for the first disciples to hear Jesus talk about his going away from them, and then to hear him say, "Apart from me you can do nothing." How was the work to go forward, how was God's agenda going to be accomplished if Jesus was going away and if without him they could do nothing?

"Nothing" is still a hard word for believers to hear today, yet Jesus also says to twenty-first-century Christians, "Apart from me you can do nothing." Apart from me, he says, you can give religious speeches, but you can't preach the gospel. Apart from me, you can hold church services, but you can't worship. Apart from me, you can put biblical and theological information in people's minds, but they won't come to faith. Apart from me, you can do church work and all kinds of good deeds, but you can't do my ministry or mission. Apart from me, you can live a virtuous life, but you can't be a Christian. This litany sounds offensive to our ears because at the top of just about any American list of virtues is a can-do spirit. Deep down, what we feel is "it's all up to us." Most Christians today would agree at least in theory that doing God's work should somehow involve God, but in practice God tends to be a distant or even absent partner.

Think, for example, about the average Presbyterian session or deacons' meeting. We have an agenda. We have individuals or committees presenting business. We have problems and issues to address. We open the meeting with prayer and perhaps a short devotional, but then we often move on with our business in much the same manner as the board of any civic association. Suggesting that God might be a very present and active participant in the proceedings of a session or deacons' meeting would be as incongruous to many officers as suggesting that one of the portraits of long-dead pastors on the wall of the session room might come to life and begin to speak. What difference would it make in our church meetings if we took very seriously the words of Jesus, "Apart from me you can do nothing"?

Strangely enough, the circumstances that drive congregations to near paralysis have great spiritual potential. In a rowboat church, as long as the church is able to keep rowing, people are often reluctant to do anything else. Rowing means that we are in control; we are getting the job done. When we get to the point when we can't row anymore or when rowing is not getting us where we need to go, then we are faced with a choice. One option is to give up. Some congregations simply run out of people or money or energy and close the doors. Many presbyteries have mercifully put dwindling, drifting churches out of their misery. Other congregations, however, decide to try doing church in a new way and become sailboat congregations. Sailboat congregations know that they cannot make the wind blow, but they do realize that they can tap into spiritual resources beyond themselves by reorienting their efforts and catching the wind of the Spirit.

This brings us to the second reality by which sailboat congregations live. We hear it in the angel Gabriel's response to Mary's question,

"How can this be, since I am a virgin?" Gabriel's response is elegantly simple: "For nothing will be impossible with God" (Luke 1:34, 37).

Sailboat churches know that when God becomes the chief guide and power source in their life and ministry, the unthinkable moves into the realm of the possible. The first believers in Jesus thought his story was finished when they put his dead body in a tomb and rolled a stone in front of the opening, but God had other possibilities in mind. Just as human will did not produce Jesus, neither did human powers have the last word on his life. He came to bring a new reign of God upon the earth that no human power could ever equal or destroy. The church was created to be both a demonstration of this new creation and a staging ground for partnering with God in taking it out to the world. Only congregations that are living into a transforming relationship with the God for whom nothing is impossible can hope to fulfill their potential as the body of Christ.

Living between the realities of "apart from me you can do nothing" and "with God all things are possible" is humbling. We acknowledge that Jesus Christ is truly the Lord and head of the church in every way, and we are powerless to do the work of his church without him. At the same time, we need to believe that the wind of Christ's Spirit still blows in the world and to have the courage to put up the sails and let God set our course. In many ways, sailing is just as hard as rowing. The difference is that rowers are confined to the power they can generate themselves; sailors learn to let the boundless power of the wind move them where they need to go.

The rest of this book is about learning to be sailors in a sailboat church. It is about living in the creative tension between our weakness and God's power, between our poverty and the wealth of resources God provides to those who humbly seek to do God's will. Being a leader in this kind of church means that your own life will also be transformed. Jesus told people who wanted to be disciples, "Those who would come after me must deny self, take up their cross, and follow me." We do not have to be miserable all the time. Rather, like Mary, we open ourselves fully to the mysterious purposes of God, even though we don't understand God's plan. God may lead us to places we would just as soon not go or use us to speak God's truth in situations of injustice where we would rather be silent. Being faithful to the crucified One may bring us trouble and struggle. However, as we give ourselves to this call, God promises to take what we give and do more with it than we could ever ask or imagine.

QUESTIONS FOR THOUGHT AND DISCUSSION

1. What do you think Jesus meant when he said, "The one who believes in me will also do the works that I do and, in fact, will do greater works than these, because I am going to the Father" (John 14:12)?

2. How do you react to the idea of church as an adventure with God? In what ways is your congregation engaged in this kind of adventure?

3. What difference would it make in your session or deacons' meetings if you took very seriously the words of Jesus "Apart from me you can do nothing"?

4. When have you observed a church operating as a rowboat? as a sailboat?

5. How do you see the Holy Spirit at work in your congregation?

4

Putting Up the Sails

Being church in a new way has three basic components—three attitudes and practices—that work together: passion for God, faith in God's provision, and willingness to let go. These attitudes and practices allow God's Spirit to take the church where God wants it to go in the same way that the interaction between wind and sails moves a boat through the water.

A PASSION FOR GOD

"Passion" can be a scary word. In a religious setting it may conjure up images of worshipers shouting, waving their hands in the air, and falling on the floor. It may revive unpleasant memories of being cornered by someone and grilled passionately about your religious beliefs. "Passion" has overtones of the style of religion some people joined the Presbyterian Church to escape. However, in terms of our relationship with God, the essence of passion is not emotion or fanaticism but commitment. To be passionate about God means that we are committed to loving God with all our heart, mind, soul, and strength and to loving our neighbor as we love ourselves. This passion for God is the first and most important sail to be hoisted in the sailboat church.

We live in a culture that devalues commitment. Loyalties that used to be considered permanent, such as commitment to a marriage or to a company, are now widely seen as temporary and disposable. Instead of commitments, our culture seems to favor contracts. A contract signifies a deal between two parties with each agreeing to do certain things. When you sign a contract to buy a house, you agree to give the owner of the house money. The owner agrees in exchange to give you the deed to the property. If either party fails to carry out its side of the bargain, the contract is broken.

A commitment goes beyond the limits of a contract and incorporates relationship. Scripture shows us a God who delights in relationship with human beings. Relationship is the very essence of who God is. God has committed to an everlasting relationship with humanity; this commitment is called a covenant. God made a covenant with Abraham to bless him and to make him a blessing to the world (Gen. 12:1–3). God was faithful to this relationship even though Abraham doubted God afterward and acted faithlessly. God also made a covenant with the people of Israel before they entered the promised land. Even when they turned away from God and worshiped idols, God did not cast them off but sent the prophets to call them back into relationship. The prophets held out hope for a day when God would make a new covenant with the people. On this day, God says, "I will put my law within them, and I will write it on their hearts" (Jer. 31:33). This new covenant would produce a people passionately committed to God from the inside out.

We cannot make ourselves have this kind of commitment to God any more than the Israelites could. Our natural sinful inclination is to push God away and do what seems good to us. A passionate, committed relationship with God is a gift that comes to us through the redeeming work of Jesus Christ and the power of the Holy Spirit. Part of what happens when the Spirit begins to work in a person is that God starts moving to the center of his or her life. Before this point, for many people, even believers, God has been on the edges of life, with one's self at the center. The little religion we have makes life a little better, like an accessory added to an outfit or a bit of spice stirred into a recipe. Spirituality makes us feel better, and so we try to fit it in when we have time, but God's impact on the deepest concerns, values, and decisions of our lives is minimal.

As the Spirit begins to work in us, the relationship with God that used to be a nice accessory in our life becomes more and more central to who we are. What God wants moves to the top of our priority list. Prayer becomes a desire more than a duty. Gratitude for God's goodness comes out of nowhere and surprises us. We hear God speak in Scripture in deeper and more personal ways. God's call on our life becomes central. Spiritual passion is about this kind of deep relationship with God that influences every area of life.

The ultimate picture of such passionate commitment is painted for us in the biblical accounts of Jesus' life. His relationship with the one he called "Abba" was at the very center of who he was, the true north of his life. Everything he did or said grew out of that relationship. After long days of teaching and healing—so busy that he did not even have time to eat—Jesus went apart from the disciples to a solitary place to pray, sometimes praying all night. He did this because he craved communion with the One who sent him into the world to serve. He was able to do what he did because of the love and power that flowed into him through this relationship.

We also see Jesus' passion in the Garden of Gethsemane. As he faced the shadow of the cross he prayed, "Father, if you are willing, remove this cup from me." He did not want to go to the cross. He did not want to suffer. Yet after struggling with these desires, he prayed, "Not my will but yours be done" (Luke 22:42). Here we see the cost of passionate commitment to God. It involves a willingness to suffer pain or loss for the sake of the relationship, and giving over control of our lives to the One who gave us life and promises us life eternal. This kind of commitment makes a person desire to seek and to do God's will no matter what that may turn out to be. In its ultimate form, as we see in the lives of the martyrs, this commitment even takes precedence over the desire to live. Leaders who are in this kind of vital relationship with the living God find what they need to lead others as they themselves are being led.

FAITH IN GOD'S PROVISION

The Bible speaks of faith as "the assurance of things hoped for, the conviction of things not seen" (Heb. 11:1). This kind of faith in God and God's promises is another essential sail to be raised in the sailboat church. It also makes a crucial difference in how church leaders carry out church business.

Let's observe, for example, the session of First Presbyterian Church as it comes together in December for its annual work-on-the-budget meeting. First, the treasurer makes the financial report and gives the session a figure for expected income for the coming year. She projects that giving will be down because some members have died and others are moving and leaving the church. The session spends the next three hours trying to figure out how to keep all the current programs going and also pay the bills for staff and utilities on less income than last year. The tone of the meeting becomes bleak as the night goes on. Tempers are strained as each frustrated elder competes for the share of the shrinking dollar pool needed to keep his or her committee's work going. Many leave the meeting depressed and wondering why they had ever thought serving on the session of their church was a good idea.

This session is engaging in what might be called money-in-the-bank thinking. Rowboat churches think about resources for ministry in this way—basing the design for the future life and mission of the church almost entirely on the present reality. The starting point and determining factor in their planning is what is in hand at the moment or will be soon. For many churches, this kind of thinking governs not only finances but every area of the church's life. We look at the facilities we currently have and design a mission that can be carried out in those facilities. We count noses in the church and decide what programs our volunteer forces can handle without too much stress. The possibilities before the congregation are whittled down to what is manageable given the resources at hand. This way of functioning keeps the church well within its comfort zone. Potential for failure and the need for risk or sacrifice are minimized. The result, however, is that our vision for the future is primarily shaped by what we now lack.

If the early Christians had engaged in money-in-the-bank thinking, the church never would have left Jerusalem. Their list of assets was pitifully short. The church had no budget, no buildings, no paid staff. They did have, however, a passionate commitment to Jesus Christ and the belief that with God all things are possible. We see these assets in action shortly after Pentecost as Peter and John encounter a crippled beggar. The custom in that day for people going to or from worship was to give alms to beggars. As the disciples approached, the man asked them for money, expecting the normal handout. "But Peter said, 'I have no silver or gold, but what I have I give you; in the name of Jesus Christ of Nazareth, stand up and walk.' . . . and immediately his feet and ankles were made strong" (Acts 3:6–7). Peter's lack of funds did not keep him from ministering to this man. By faith in the risen Christ, he had access to resources far beyond the limitations of his empty pocketbook.

Leaders in a sailboat church know that money and resources are never really the issue when it comes to the church's mission. When a church is busy doing what God wants it to do, the resources will be provided. Exciting things happen in the church when leaders move away from a money-in-the-bank mentality and start focusing instead on seeking and doing God's will in everything. The Christian life was never meant to be something that we do ourselves. God desires to have a deep and intimate partnership with us in God's desire to bless the whole world. The deeper we allow God to go in our lives, the more we will experience God's guidance and provision in every area of our life, and the more we will trust God. This approach will in time change how we do business as church leaders.

In contrast to First Presbyterian, when the session of Christ Presbyterian Church met in May for their annual planning retreat, they spent some time reviewing the church's mission statement and the long- and short-term goals of their church. They evaluated how things were going in the church in light of those goals. In a time of worship and thanksgiving they celebrated the past year's achievements, such as sending a short-term mission team to Mexico and becoming a founding participant in their town's first food pantry for needy families. After worship they took time both individually and as a group to meditate on, pray over, and discuss together the question, "What is God calling our church to be and do in the coming year?" Based on what came out of this discussion and prayer, they brainstormed a number of possible new ministries, including some new projects such as renovating a house the church owned for use as transitional housing for homeless families. They also proposed a number of possibilities for expanding current ministries, including the Mexico relationship. When this work was completed, the officers took home a list of all the possibilities and covenanted to pray about them until the next meeting.

When the session met again a month later, the key question before them was, "What is God calling us to be and do in the coming year?" They began with an hour of prayer and reflection on Scripture. Then they shared and discussed the fruit of their individual meditation on the list of possible ministries from the last meeting. During this discussion some items were deleted from the list by common consent; one new possibility was added. Again, after a time of reflection and prayer for God's will to be done, elders were invited to mark their top three choices on the list of possible new or expanded ministries. Five ministries rose to the top of the list. Passionate discussion ensued regarding the choices and which were most appropriate for the next year. After listening to each other and taking several more votes, two of the possibilities emerged as ministries the great majority of session members felt the church was being led to do. As the meeting closed in worship, the elders pledged to pray together about these things in the weeks ahead.

In the meantime, each mission task group of the church was asked to make plans for the coming year based on the church's long-term and short-term goals and session's discernment of God's leading for the coming year. In August the session took these ideas and created out of them a ministry plan for the congregation for the year ahead. The ministry plan, along with how the session saw it helping to meet the congregation's goals, was used in the church's stewardship emphasis in early fall. In November the session met to formulate the budget for the new year. The meeting began with worship and prayer for guidance. The session was asked to think once again on the question, "What is it that God wants us to do this coming year?" The treasurer then made the financial report. Projected giving was down due to some members moving away.

The session had to make some hard decisions, including finding ways to do more of the clerical work of the church with volunteers instead of hiring another staff member and delaying a paint job for the sanctuary. But through it all they were guided by the goals, priorities, and ministry plan they had discerned earlier. Instead of elders competing to get their piece of the shrinking pie, the session worked together to figure out how to carry the plan forward. At the end of the meeting, the session adjourned to the sanctuary where they dedicated to God the ministry plan and budget for the coming year. Many left the sanctuary feeling excited about what God might do and were glad to have been a part of it all.

This session was raising the sail of faith in God's provision and guidance for the church's mission. Their planning process was based on the belief, or at least a strong suspicion, that God "by the power at work within us is able to accomplish abundantly far more than all we can ask or imagine" (Eph. 3:20). They knew that the burden of deciding what to do and making things happen does not rest on our shoulders alone. God guides, changes minds, overcomes resistance, provides funds, and opens doors far beyond what we can ask or imagine. When we start with a conviction about what God can do instead of focusing only on what we can do, church leadership becomes a spiritual adventure.

The guiding force for this adventure is provided by the third person of the Trinity. Jesus called the Holy Spirit "the Advocate." The root of this word means one who comes alongside to help. The Spirit is given to us at our baptism and dwells in every believer. The degree to which we will be truly effective spiritual leaders is the degree to which we invite the Holy Spirit to guide and provide resources for all we do. The Spirit works in, through, and beyond the church and individual believers to carry out God's dream for the redemption of the world. We cannot fulfill our potential as the body of Christ without allowing the Holy Spirit to guide, provide for, and transform us.

WILLINGNESS TO LET GO

A third sail that enables the wind of the Spirit to move the church along is a willingness to let go of things that get in God's way, clearing space in our lives and in the church for God to work. The list of these obstacles will differ from church to church and from person to person, of course. But if we want the wind of the Spirit to be the prime mover in our church, we must let go of two things that consistently block God: the need for control and the need for comfort.

The Need for Control

Our human need to be in control often blocks God's wishes. At the heart of this attitude is the sin that led Adam and Eve astray. Genesis tells the sad story of how the first human beings broke fellowship with God by doing what seemed good to them, contrary to God's command. They did not intentionally set out to to ruin their relationship with God; they simply wanted to be equal to God. They wanted to be in control. They wanted a life apart from God, forgetting that they were creatures and that creatures have no life apart from their Creator.

The struggle to be in control is a kind of addiction that is part of our fallen human nature. Even the most passionate lovers of God must deal with layer upon layer of what spiritual writer Thomas Merton called the false self. This is the self that is always protecting, building up, and taking care of those values, systems, people, and things that make us happy, safe, and comfortable. This is the self Satan was trying to hook when he tempted Jesus to create bread out of stones, jump off the temple roof, and worship him in exchange for the whole world. Jesus consistently turned away from this false self throughout his life, and at times his struggle was painful. In the Garden of Gethsemane, as Jesus faced the desire to save himself and avoid the cross, his agony produced sweat like great drops of blood (Luke 22:39–44).

When we stubbornly insist on our own way or treat others harshly in order to achieve our own ends, it is obvious that we are not centered on God. But a deeper truth is that even when we spend our time, energy, and money on the needs and wants of others, our false self is always ready to see what's in it for us. Any psychologist can tell stories of people who seemed to be selfless servants of others, but were actually driven by desperate needs to manipulate, please, and control. When we believe we are in control, we feel safe. When we face the reality that God is really in control, we are thrown into the realm of faith. We must trust in what we cannot yet see. In God's realm, if we do not stand by faith, we do not stand at all.

God cannot give our churches everything God wants us to have until we leaders are willing to let go of our need to be in control of the church and through faith we let God take charge. If Jesus, the Son of God, had to give up control over his life in the Garden of Gethsemane, what makes us think that God is going to take us and our churches by a different path? Actually it is a great relief to let God take God's rightful place as Lord and head of the church and take our places as junior partners in God's work. Leaders who always have to be in control, always carrying the church on their shoulders, are at serious risk for burnout.

I imagine that most of what was happening with the believers between the ascension of Jesus and Pentecost day had to do with giving up control. They had to let go of what they thought the agenda was. They had to let go of the idea that they were equipped to move into God's future. They had to feel the powerlessness of their human weakness before they could be open to receive the power of the Holy Spirit. They had to know in their deepest selves that they were only clay jars (2 Cor. 4:7) before God could pour God's treasure into them. So it was that as the wind of the Spirit began to blow on Pentecost, Peter stood before the gathered crowd and talked, not about himself or the other disciples, not about their plans or ideas, but instead about Jesus and about God's gracious work to save the world through him.

So it must be with us if we want to be engaged in the adventure of life with God. As long as we are charting the course, God cannot take us where God wants us to go. As long as we are pursuing self-generated agendas that seem good to us, God has little room to work God's agenda out among us. The bottom line is that God is meant to lead and we are meant to follow in the dance we call church. A church whose leaders act in ways that keep them firmly in control of their church's life are much more likely to end up rowing than sailing.

The Need to Be Comfortable

In order for the wind of the Spirit to carry us where God wants us to go, we also need to let go of our need to be comfortable. It is human nature to seek comfort and to flee discomfort. One of the places people may seek comfort and stability in an uncomfortable, unstable world is church. Sometimes the need for comfort causes people to resist change or anything that makes them uncomfortable. This dynamic can present an occupational hazard for church leaders: they can spend inordinate amounts of time and energy making sure that people in their church are comfortable. Keeping them comfortable prevents their complaining and doing other things that make us uncomfortable. Yet if this is the focus of our leadership, we very well may be blocking what God wants to do in and through our church.

Jesus was not a placater. He seemed to make people uncomfortable on a regular basis. He called his first disciples into an enterprise that turned their lives upside down, making them and their families very uncomfortable. He said things that often made the crowds listening to him similarly uncomfortable: "Deny yourself, take up your cross daily and follow me"; "Go sell all that you have, give it to the poor, then come and follow me"; "Give to everyone who asks of you and do not refuse those who would borrow from you"; "Love your enemies." When he overturned the tables of the businesspeople in the temple and scattered their property far and wide, he caused such discomfort in the temple that its leaders began to plan how to rid themselves of him. To follow Jesus is by definition to follow a path that regularly takes us out of our comfort zone.

Covenant Presbyterian Church experienced this need to let go of being comfortable when they invited an immigrant fellowship composed of Spanish-speaking Presbyterians to worship on Sunday afternoons in their church building. The session of Covenant Church felt that it was God's will and a good thing all around for the two groups to share an underused building. The two groups slowly grew to know each other and enjoy their relationship. They worshiped together occasionally and cooperated to offer a vacation Bible school to the neighborhood.

However, in time, their cultural and language differences, and the different needs of the two ministries, began to create friction. While still agreeing that the relationship was a good thing, the elders grew increasingly frustrated with having to manage so many changes. In spite of everyone's best efforts, problems kept popping up, and people were irritated. The Covenant Church's session meetings became places to air these tensions.

At one such session meeting an astute elder said, "We do have quite a few issues to work out with our Spanish-speaking friends, but these kinds of relationships are always going to involve some give-and-take on all sides. Part of our problem is that we are expecting things to be just like they were when we were in these buildings by ourselves. That's not a reasonable expectation! These problems do make us uncomfortable. They do require extra effort on the part of everyone. But isn't that a small price to pay for all the blessings we receive from this relationship?"

This elder was challenging the session to let go of being as comfortable as they once were in order to be sailboat Christians. His remarks refocused the situation for the session, and they once again committed themselves wholeheartedly to doing what it would take to make the relationship work with the Spanish-speaking fellowship. Generally speaking, human nature is averse to this kind of sacrifice. It will only come to pass as the Holy Spirit enables us to let go of our need to be comfortable and gives us the ability to move with the wind.

The wind of the Spirit is blowing today just as much as when the first believers sailed out to make disciples of all nations. God has everything we need to be faithful in our mission and discipleship, and God is more than willing to give it to us as we humbly allow ourselves to be moved by God's Spirit. Pray for a deeper passion for God, for more faith to claim God's resources, and for a willingness to let go of everything that is blocking God's will. Raise up the sails! As you do, you and your church will be empowered.

QUESTIONS FOR THOUGHT AND DISCUSSION

1. Draw a circle representing your life. Make a mark in the circle representing how close God is to the center of your life. How does this relationship with God empower your ministry as a church officer?
2. How much quality time do you generally spend paying attention to God each day? Each week?
3. How do you see money-in-the-bank thinking at work in your church? When have you seen the church move beyond it in faith?
4. Tell about a time when you had to move outside your comfort zone to be faithful to God.

5

Sailing Skills for Church Leaders

USING SANCTIFIED IMAGINATION

There are hundreds of good things that we could be doing at any given time, numberless needs in the world that could be addressed in God's name. But not all of those are necessarily our personal responsibility as individuals or congregations. God means for us to take on some needs while other needs constitute a calling for some other church. Part of the work of spiritual leadership is to help the congregation to discern its particular calling and mission and to imagine what shape it might take. Sometimes the answer is surprising.

In the mid-1980s, Clifton Presbyterian Church in Atlanta discerned a call to ministry among the city's increasing number of homeless people. After much prayer and discussion, it decided to begin a night shelter at the church. The surprising thing about this decision was that the congregation at that time had about thirty members and was meeting in a smallish house that had been remodeled into a church building. The church had no special funding, few volunteers, and limited facilities. Yet each evening members of the church began going to the inner city in their own cars and transporting homeless men back to the church. There they were given a warm welcome, a hot meal, and a safe place to sleep on the floor of the sanctuary. It wasn't easy to keep the ministry going; obstacles arose. However, other churches in the presbytery started to send volunteers and money. People in the neighborhood came to see the ministry as a good thing, and slowly a cadre of neighbors emerged to take part in the work and give financial support. So began the first night shelter for homeless people in the city of Atlanta.

This particular ministry came into being because the leadership of the congregation was able to envision what faithfulness to God looked like in its particular and unique place. The leaders used their Holy Spirit–led imagination to see beyond what was to what could be. Effective spiritual leaders are able to take the general principles of the faith, hold those up against the context in which they live, and ask, "What will it look like for us to be faithful to God in this place, at this time?" They can make the mental jump from abstract to concrete, from the principle to the living embodiment of the principle. They look at their aging neighbors and imagine a senior center in the church. They see street children in the Congo on television and imagine joining with other churches to start an orphanage there. They see increasing numbers of unchurched people under thirty in their area and imagine a worship service appealing especially to them. As they let the Holy Spirit work in their imagination, God uses them to bring this world a little closer to what God wants it to be. The important thing is not how smart we are, but rather how open we are to the still, small voice of the Spirit.

It could be argued that the malaise in many churches today is at least partly due to a failure of imagination. When we cannot imagine God doing a new thing among us, the energy and excitement go out of church life. We tend to spend our time continuing the past or holding on to the present. Neither is it enough only to believe in theory that God is able to do new and exciting things in our midst, for God calls us to be active partners in the adventure. Effective spiritual leaders will always be asking God what the repentant crowds asked John the Baptist: "What then should we do?" In answer, God enables the faithful to dream dreams and see visions.

By advocating the use of sanctified imagination, I'm not implying that leaders are justified in acting like loose cannons, rampaging through the church doing whatever comes into their minds. The appropriate use of this spiritual gift is rooted in a deep sense of, first, what it entails to be Jesus' disciples and, second, a clear understanding of what Christian faithfulness means and has meant in times past. A firm grounding in Scripture is also essential, not so that we can quote reams of Scripture from memory, but rather that we are so steeped in the full witness of Scripture that it shapes how we think, act, and make decisions. Instead of using Scripture to further our ends, we must have the humility to let Scripture judge and transform us.

In the Presbyterian Church (U.S.A.), leaders must also honor the boundaries provided by our constitution: the *Book of Confessions* and the *Book of Order*. The *Book of Confessions* reminds us that we are not the first Christians who ever lived. Others before us have wrestled with the demands of the gospel and left us their testimony. these voices from the past help us understand true faithfulness. Similarly, The *Book of Order* is the distilled wisdom of our denomination regarding how the church should operate. Both parts of the constitution provide valuable resources to help us "test the spirits to see whether they are from God" (1 John 4:1).

RISING ABOVE SELF-INTEREST FOR THE GOOD OF THE CHURCH

Parents will tell you that raising children often involves sacrificing your desires for their sake. You get up for the 2 a.m. feeding when you would much rather stay in bed. You would love to sit down with the paper when you get home from work, but instead you take your child to soccer practice. You may prefer a sporty new car, but you buy the cheaper used model and put the difference into the savings account for college. Parents are called to rise above their own self-interest and preferences when necessary in the interest of their children. Leaders are often called to do the same thing in regard to the church.

Ironically, popular images of leadership often involve using power to get what one wants. The chauffeured limo, the generous expense account, the first-class airplane seat, assistants at one's beck and call—these are the signs of a successful leader in the political or economic arena. This situation was essentially the same in Jesus' day. After breaking up an argument over which of the disciples would sit in seats of power at his right and left hands, Jesus reminded them, "The rulers of the Gentiles lord it over them, and their great ones are tyrants. . . . It will not be so among you; but whoever wishes to be great among you must be your servant, and whoever wishes to be first among you must be your slave; just as the Son of Man came not to be served but to serve, and to give his life a ransom for many" (Matt. 20:25–28). Effective spiritual leaders know that being a leader does not always mean having one's own way. At times we must give up what we want for the good of others or to further the mission of the church.

The need to rise above personal preference can even involve such issues as the use of church space. People tend to be territorial about their church buildings, often because, over time, the experiences we have in certain spaces tend to fill those places with special meaning. The Sunday school room, the choir room, the parlor, and the sanctuary can become holy ground because they are full of memories we hold dear. These feelings are natural and are part of the glue that holds us to the church. Problems arise, however, when the desire to use or control what happens in certain spaces stands in the way of the church's mission.

Eastside Presbyterian Church faced this issue when it ran out of rooms for Sunday school classes. A Bible study class for new Christians had met for a while in the pastor's study, but before long, the class outgrew the space and needed a new place to meet. When the education committee convened to deal with this issue, members discovered that the smallest adult class in the church was meeting in the largest classroom. This group, the Couples Class, had been meeting in the same room for more than forty years. In the beginning the group had more than fifty members, all young married people who came together during the education hour every week. They made up the biggest class in the church and needed the largest room to accommodate everyone. Over time, however, members died or moved away. Now on a Sunday morning, the Couples Class averaged six to eight in Sunday school, but still met in the large room.

The president of the class was serving on the session. While sad at the thought of leaving a room filled with so many good memories, she understood the need to find space for the new class. She initiated a meeting with the pastor and the chair of the education committee and presented the problem; she suggested that before the classroom switch took place, they honor the history of the Couples Class and give its members opportunity to share this history with others. The pastor then met with the class and presented the need, helping them understand the importance of their sacrifice and offering his study as a new meeting space.

On the day the room switch was made, the Couples Class served brunch to the group taking over its former classroom. The pastor introduced the new members to the Couples Class members, and then the Couples Class members told stories about the people and events that made that space holy ground for them. The elder who had helped make the move possible closed the program with a prayer for God to bless both groups in their new meeting rooms. This elder had the ability to rise above personal feelings and to help others do so for the greater good of the church. In many situations of potential conflict, this type of approach makes all the difference.

Personal preferences are also an issue when it comes to worship. Many churches today are in conflict over the form of their worship service; congregations have even split over the differences. In negotiating what has been called "the worship wars,"[1] it is important to understand that much of the furor is about style rather than substance. The controversy often turns on one group's preference for a formal or more traditional service with organ music and songs sung out of a hymnal and another's for something less traditional, perhaps a more free-flowing service with contemporary songs led by a praise team or band.

Unfortunately, battle lines are sometimes drawn around these preferences. People who want a more informal style of worship may feel hurt and angry when others react negatively to their requests for change. The choir director, organist, or choir may feel threatened when asked to lead, sing, or play music they don't like. Those who prefer contemporary music may complain that they aren't being spiritually fed by hymns from the hymnal. The preacher may be afraid of being asked to preach a more informal sermon without a pulpit or notes. None of these reactions have to do with the essence of worship itself—that the gospel is truly preached and God is rightly glorified. Rather they grow out of the natural human desire to have things the way we like them, especially at church.

To resolve conflict like this, effective spiritual leaders must work together to discern what style of worship and configuration of worship services best further the mission of the church, and in the process they must rise above their own personal desires and preferences for worship. The session of Main Street Presbyterian Church came to realize that its parish included thousands of students living on the campus of a nearby university. They'd tried repeatedly to attract the students to their traditional 11 a.m. service, but their efforts bore little fruit. But then, one night, a seminary intern suggested starting a Tuesday night service with music provided by a band. He invited members of the session to attend such a service at another church, and a few weeks later about half the session boarded the church van to see what this new kind of service was all about.

At the next session meeting, discussion was lively. "I could hardly wait to get out of there," said one elder. "The music gave me a headache." Another elder noted that the room had been overflowing with college students and that they seemed to respond enthusiastically to the pastor's sermon. As the discussion turned to the possibility of having a similar service at their own church, one of the older elders spoke: "I hate that kind of music, and I would probably never come to this new service. But if doing this might help us reach young people that we might not otherwise reach for Christ, I am all for it." His comment helped focus the session's attention on the mission of the church instead of on personal preferences about music.

This kind of leadership involves humility of spirit, requiring that we realize that just because something is right for us does not mean it is right for everyone; just because we prefer doing things a certain way does not mean that is always the best way to do it. Such leadership involves the ability to stand back and look at the big picture when making decisions instead of always doing what we would prefer. Sometimes it may mean sacrificing our own personal desires and interests so that the mission of the church may go forward. Effective spiritual leaders are willing to rise above self-interest and personal preference for the greater good of the whole. In so doing they follow the example of Jesus, who came not to be served, but to serve.

THE WILLINGNESS TO RISK AND FAIL

The Gospel of Matthew tells the parable of the Talents. The story is about a man who entrusts to three of his servants large amounts of money (a talent was worth about fifteen years of wages for a laborer). Then he goes away on a long journey. When he returns, he calls the servants for an accounting. Two of the servants have used the money left in their charge to make a profit for the master. They are praised and rewarded. The third servant, however, motivated by fear, has buried the master's money in the ground for safekeeping. He comes before the master bringing back the money he had been given, expecting no doubt to receive a commendation for returning the talent safe and sound. Instead, he gets a scathing rebuke and is thrown "into the outer darkness where there will be weeping and gnashing of teeth" (Matt. 25:14–30).

What did this third servant do wrong? He did not lose the money. He did not waste it in drinking and gambling. He did not risk the money in uncertain investments or let thieves steal it. What did this unfortunate man do to incur the rage of the master? The story seems to say that his sin was in conserving the talent. He was judged harshly, not for losing the talent, but for failing to try to do anything with it. He felt that his primary job was to save what the master had entrusted to him.

His nightmare was losing it. Fear of failure kept him from taking a risk with what he had been given, and for this lack of action he was thrown into the outer darkness.

Those who are in positions of spiritual leadership need to be clear about the content of their call. What are we to be doing in God's name, and what does it mean to be successful? Our culture holds out a particular image of success. It's big and profitable, and it involves positive numbers and positive cash flow. To succeed is to be a star, a hit, a winner. Success is victory, triumph, and achievement. Failure is their absence.

If we look to the life of Jesus for a definition of success, however, we see a different picture. By the world's measure he never achieved success in his work and died a failure at a relatively young age. Jesus had every opportunity and all the gifts necessary to succeed, according to the world's definition. But he chose another way. Jesus never saw his mission through the lens of worldly success. He knew his call was to be faithful to God and to God's will. In a strange way, Jesus succeeded by failing, which is the mystery of the cross. In his obedient death, a great failure and scandal in the eyes of his contemporaries, he reached ultimate success in faithfulness to God.

Many churches wither and die because their leaders are afraid of trying and failing. Like the third servant in the parable, they are afraid to take the risks necessary to do the Master's will. God is always going ahead of us, doing new things and inviting us to join in. Trying something new usually involves the possibility that it may not work. Investing in new ministries may call for a significant outlay of money without any guarantee of return. Leaders who are addicted to success cannot abide the possibility of failure, so rather than risk losing what God has given to the church, they turn into guardians of a building, a balanced budget, a tradition, or an endowment. Rather than being in mission, their main responsibility becomes protecting and conserving the church's assets.

Effective spiritual leaders know that in the church, success is about faithfulness, and faithfulness sometimes requires taking risks. These leaders know that God calls us to walk by faith and not by sight, and they are willing to call their congregations to take a leap of faith when it seems necessary to do God's will. In all this, the attitude of the leaders makes a major difference in how their congregation reacts to uncertainty and risk. When leaders are worried about failure, the members will probably also be reluctant to stretch far outside their comfort zone. If the leaders are fearful and tense, the congregation will begin to see itself as fragile and in danger. Fear and insecurity are contagious.

Effective leadership involves having the faith to be a nonanxious presence in the midst of anxiety-producing situations. To the congregation's fearful questions, such a leader might answer, "We are going to try something new. We don't really know whether it will work or not. We won't know that until we try it. But we believe this is what God wants us to do, so we are going to take a leap of faith and go ahead. If it doesn't work out, we will try something else, and we will have learned a lot in the process." But of course the leader herself must believe that.

The *Book of Order* says, "The Church is called to be a sign in and for the world of the new reality which God has made available to people in Jesus Christ. . . . [It] is called to undertake this mission even at the risk of losing its life, trusting in God alone as the author and giver of life" (G-3.0200a, 3.0400).

The goal of being an effective leader requires a willingness to risk what God has given for the sake of doing God's will. The risks may involve the church's finances, the church's buildings, or even the church's reputation in the community, which can be a frightening call. But those who are willing in faith to take the risk will receive the commendation of the Master: "Well done, good and faithful servant!"

THE ABILITY TO DISCERN AND USE THE GIFTS OF OTHERS IN GOD'S WORK

The New Testament shows us a church that practiced what might be called charismatic leadership. The root of the word "charismatic" is the Greek word *charis*, which means gift. The apostle Paul explains to the Corinthian church that God gives spiritual gifts to the members of the church to empower the church for its mission (1 Cor. 12:4–11).

In today's church, unfortunately, the expectation often seems to be that all the spiritual gifts the congregation needs will be concentrated in the pastor. This is not a biblical idea, and when it is put into practice it can do serious damage to a church's health. The truth is that every single church member has gifts for ministry. When a high proportion of members actively put their gifts to work toward God's mission for that church, the church tends to be healthy. When, in contrast, all the gifts must come from the pastor, or perhaps the pastor and a few leaders, the church suffers. For this reason, effective leadership involves helping people find their spiritual gifts and encouraging them to put these gifts to work for God's sake.

Instead of helping members find their ministries, however, many churches settle for recruiting warm bodies to hold positions. "How many slots do we have to fill?" is often the guiding question for nominating and other committees. We often draft people to do things for which they have no gifts or inclination, just to meet institutional quotas. In taking this action, we sometimes set them up to fail. Without a doubt, we deny them the joy of discovering and using the special gifts God gave them for ministry.

While many Christians can tell stories of volunteering to do something absolutely foreign to their gifts and experience and finding that the Spirit equipped them as they went along, another pattern seems to be that God places people and gifts in the church to carry forward the kinds of mission God wants to happen there. For example, a church with many people who love to teach could start an after-school program or a Bible study ministry in the local jail. A church with seasoned people of prayer might consider a ministry of intercession and healing. A church with many folks who have the gift of hospitality could sponsor refugee families. The possibilities are endless, but the point is to help people find and use the gifts that God has given them.

Exciting things can happen if, instead of slotting people into jobs to keep on doing what your church has always done before, the church's mission is shaped at least partly around the gifts God has given its members. It may feel risky at first; some positions might not get filled. You may, however, discover new energy bubbling up in your congregation as people experience the joy of employing their God-given gifts.

Joyfulness happens partly because serving in ministry and mission is a major avenue of spiritual growth. Service intensifies a person's dependence on God and opens up deeper avenues of prayer and commitment. The shift from doing institutional maintenance to being in ministry for God also tends to attract new people into the active core of the church. People who would never agree to serve on the session or a committee can find their place doing something active to forward the ministry of their church. Even homebound people can have a ministry of prayer or give pastoral care over the telephone. Ministries and gifts are varied, but the one Spirit is in all of them and will touch the lives of those who are trying to use their gifts in God's service.

Elders and deacons are in a great position to function as spiritual fruit harvesters in the congregation. How? They do it in two steps. First, they keep their eyes open to see the giftedness in others, and then they use sanctified imagination to see where these gifts might be used in

God's service. This responsibility can be churchwide and more organized as well. Some churches, for example, regularly use a spiritual gifts inventory with their new members as a way of helping them to find their ministry in the congregation. Such an exercise could also be part of confirmation classes. Other churches make the discernment and commitment of spiritual gifts a regular part of their year-round stewardship emphasis. At some time during the year, but not during the financial pledge season, they encourage members to look seriously at their gifts and make a pledge of time to a particular ministry in or through the church. If your church does this, make sure that the commitments are followed up on and that people are put to work.

In many churches 20 percent of the people do 80 percent of the work. Often that 20 percent is overburdened and weary, and the 80 percent tend to be passive consumers of the programs and ministries provided by the pastor and the other 20 percent. Effective spiritual leaders cannot be satisfied with this way of doing church. Rather, they must work toward the goal of having every member involved in ministry that feeds and challenges them to the end that the mission of the church will go forward and God will be glorified.

USING THE RESOURCES OF TRADITION AND HISTORY

Every occupation has a collection of tools that are instrumental in getting the work done. No self-respecting chef would work in a kitchen without a set of sharp knives. When the plumber shows up to fix your leaky fixtures, she has a good selection of wrenches at her disposal. The doctor has a stethoscope; the lawyer has law books. So it is also with officers in the Presbyterian Church. Our essential tools include knowledge of the church's Scripture, theology, polity, and history. To be an effective spiritual leader, you must be able to access all these resources in ways that validate and shape the mission of the church.

The most important resource is Scripture. At their ordination all officers are asked, "Will you fulfill your office in obedience to Jesus Christ, *under the authority of Scripture?*" (G-14.0207d, emphasis added). Scripture is at the heart of our faith. All the Reformed confessions point in one way or another to Scripture as the "rule of faith and life."[2] Trying to lead the church of Jesus Christ without the guidance of Scripture would be like trying to drive a car with a bag over your head. The challenge faced by those who take this high understanding of Scripture seriously is how we interpret Scripture and understand its authority.

The Reformed tradition maintains that Scripture is authoritative in matters relating to our knowledge of God, salvation, and faithful living. The Westminster Shorter Catechism declares, "The Scriptures principally teach what man is to believe concerning God, and what duty God requires of man."[3] Scripture should be our first touchstone as we try to discern how to please God and how to lead the people of God. While we may listen to many voices in our search for truth, for Presbyterians, Scripture is the first and last voice we hear.

Responsible leaders should be engaged in regular and serious study of Scripture to grow in faith and wisdom. They will want to read what trustworthy scholars say about the original language and setting of Scripture. They will take pains always to understand a particular Scripture text in its historical and literary context. They will try to have a sense of what God's word was to the first readers of the Scripture as well as what God might be trying to say to them today. In the matter of interpreting Scripture, our Reformed branch of the Christian church has always held that God gave human beings a brain and expects us to use it. For this reason we encourage scholarship and generally require our ordained pastors to go to seminary, and it is also why we encourage everyone in the church to be engaged in some kind of group Bible study on a regular basis, whether in a church school class, a circle, or a weekday Bible study and prayer group.

Above all, leaders who want to be led by Scripture seek the guidance of the Holy Spirit as they try to interpret it. The Scots Confession states, "When controversy arises about the right understanding of any passage or sentence of Scripture . . . we ought not so much to ask what men have said or done before us, as what the Holy Ghost uniformly speaks within the body of the Scriptures and what Christ Jesus himself did and commanded."[4] John Calvin also affirmed the importance of the Spirit in our hearing and interpreting God's Word when he wrote: "For by a kind of mutual bond the Lord has joined the certainty of his word and of his Spirit so that the perfect religion of the Word may abide in our minds when the Spirit, who causes us to contemplate God's face, shines."[5] Officers who want to be equipped for their work as leaders will sit with the Word of God on a regular basis both to study it and to listen for the Spirit's voice speaking in it.

The theology and history of the church are also helpful tools for leaders. Taken together, the documents in our *Book of Confessions* contain a basic library of Reformed Christian theology. They show us how Christians in times past interpreted Scripture to face the challenges of their day. Their testimony is helpful to us as we seek to follow in their footsteps. Knowledge of church history can also give us a wider perspective from which to make faithful decisions about the church's life. For instance, in some congregations issues around the frequency and method of serving Communion are controversial: Should it be once a quarter, once a month, or once a week? Should it be served in the pew or should people go up to the front? How about dipping the bread in a common cup versus having the cup served in little glasses? The church has responded to all of these issues over the centuries, and rich layers of theological meaning surround their interpretations. Wise leaders seek the assistance of Scripture, theology, and history rather than relying on their own tastes and preferences.

Another important tool for church leaders is even closer at hand: knowledge of the history and traditions of your local church. One way to validate and affirm your church's current mission is to find ways to connect it to significant events and people in its past. Make a point of soliciting and reflecting on the stories the congregation tells about itself and its history. One session discovered the power of this history when it felt led to propose that the church begin a day-care ministry. They saw this step as a possible way of connecting with younger families moving into their neighborhood. This particular ministry was a stretch for the congregation and entailed significant financial commitment and risk. The session expected opposition to the proposal, but when the idea was presented for the first time, the older members of the church became its advocates. They were the ones who could remember that back in the 1950s, when many young couples with children were moving into their neighborhood, the church drew many of them into the congregation through a very successful child-care program. They were willing to take a risk on a new ministry because they remembered a time in their history when another such program was a blessing to the church.

Finally, our Presbyterian form of church government (polity) is also a resource for spiritual leadership. Theological themes basic to our faith are woven into our life together through the structure of our denomination's church government. One of the promises every ordained officer of the PC(USA) makes upon his or her ordination and installation is to be governed by our church's polity and to abide by its discipline (G-14.0207e). The *Book of Order* contains the PC(USA)'s Form of Government, Directory for Worship, and Rules of Discipline. These documents seek to shape our communal life in accord with Scripture. As you seek to be a faithful spiritual leader in a Presbyterian church, our polity provides essential theological touchstones for you.

One of these, the doctrine of the sovereignty of God, reminds us whose we are and to whom the church belongs. Sovereignty is a political term relating to the right to rule. Sovereign nations have the right to enforce their political will within their boundaries. Presbyterians use this term to talk about God's relationship to God's creation. God is sovereign over the earth and everything in it because God is the creator of the universe. God has the right to rule by virtue of the fact that "the earth is the LORD's and all that is in it, the world, and those who live in it; for he has founded it on the seas, and established it on the rivers" (Ps. 24:1–2). When human beings broke fellowship with God, in the fullness of time, God sent his only son to reestablish right relationship between God and God's creation. The church exists because of the death, resurrection, and ascension of Jesus Christ; he is sovereign—the Lord and head of the church. As leaders in the church we must always be aware that we have a mission from Christ to carry out. Our Form of Government reminds us that the church is to pursue this mission "even at the risk of losing its life, trusting in God alone as the author and giver of life" (G-3.0400).

Another of these theological touchstones, the doctrine of the unity of the church, reminds us how we should live together. Unity in the church can seem a very elusive thing. Differences of opinion over how to interpret Scripture, how to conduct worship, and how to live the Christian life have created division in the Christian church from the beginning. Our own denomination has struggled with a variety of issues from its early days even until now with each round of theological conflict making the prospect of unity look ever more dim.

Our *Book of Order* reminds us in no uncertain terms that we do not create the unity of the church. Christian unity is not based upon our agreement on theological questions. Instead our unity is based on the work of Jesus Christ in gathering a people to himself. There is only one body of Christ in this world, and it is made up of "all persons in every nation, together with their children, who profess faith in Jesus Christ as Lord and Savior and commit themselves to live in a fellowship under his rule" (G-4.0101).

The church is not simply a voluntary association like a service club or sports league. At the deepest level we are a body that is organically bound together by the blood of Christ. Our unity as Christians is already a reality, a gift from God. Our call is to live into that unity even when our brothers and sisters anger us and our differences seem insurmountable. Presbyterian polity—structured as a system of interlinking relationships—gives us resources for that work and helps us stay faithful to Christ and to each other.

A deep understanding of sin and grace is another theological touchstone woven into our form of church government. Presbyterians understand the reality of sin and know that if left to our own devices, human beings generally do our own will instead of God's will. Even the redeemed saints of God who are being sanctified by the Holy Spirit are prone to sin and must live by God's grace and forgiveness. Provisions are built into the *Book of Order* to deal with sin in the body of Christ. They include a system of checks and balances between church governing bodies, an insistence on communal decision making, and a disciplinary process to provide just and efficient settlement of differences. These facts of our polity are not seen as necessary evils but rather as means of grace for the church as it seeks to reflect the light of Christ into the world.

DISCERNING THE *KAIROS* MOMENTS

Biblical Greek has two words that are translated as the word "time." One is *chronos*, indicating time as measured by a clock or calendar. This kind of time governs when we wake up in the morning and go to bed at night, pick up the children from school, and show up for our doctor's appointment. *Chronos* is the time that governs our daily lives. The Bible also talks about *kairos* time. *Kairos* refers to both a special season of life when certain actions are appropriate or to a time of exceptional opportunity from God.[6]

It is important to develop sensitivity to these *kairos* moments, the spiritual times and seasons in the life of the church. The writer of Ecclesiastes says, "For everything there is a season, and a time for every matter under heaven" (Eccl. 3:1), and then catalogs a variety of events in life that each has its own special time. The idea here is that certain activities are appropriate at certain seasons or times, and others are not. If your church has suffered many losses, it may be the season to grieve. If a new building has been built or the church is commemorating a major anniversary, it is time to celebrate. Sometimes a church needs to draw inward and pay close attention to its communal life. Then there are times when focusing major energy in mission outside the congregation is appropriate. The context of your congregation provides the clues about what is appropriate for a particular time in your church's life. God issues particular challenges and opportunities for a congregation in each *kairos* season.

Timing is also extremely important when it comes to birthing new programs and ministries in the church. Those who have delivered children into the world can testify that there is a time to let nature take its course and then there is a time to push. Pushing too soon can injure the baby. The same holds true in trying to bring something new into the life of a church. There are seasons when proposals need to germinate in the minds and hearts of people. There are times to move plans along slowly, allowing everyone to get on board, and then the time comes to act swiftly and decisively to move an idea to fulfillment. Through prayer, reflection on Scripture, consultation with others, and paying attention to the movement of the Holy Spirit in the church, effective spiritual leaders learn to sense when to push through and when to hold back.

Another facet of the meaning of *kairos* refers to that special, holy time when God presents human beings with an exceptional opportunity. The first words out of Jesus' mouth in the Gospel of Mark are "The time is fulfilled, and the kingdom of God has come near; repent, and believe in the good news" (Mark 1:15). Jesus' presence among us on earth was the ultimate *kairos* moment. He held open the door of God's kingdom, and people were obliged either to enter or to turn away. There is no place for neutrality when such times come.

Jesus shows us the impact *kairos* moments have on people in two familiar parables in Matthew. In Matthew 13:44, a man finds a hidden treasure in a field, "then in his joy he goes and sells all that he has and buys that field." Another man, a pearl merchant, "on finding one pearl of great value, he went and sold all that he had and bought it" (Matt. 13:45–46). The kingdom of heaven, Jesus says, is like these amazing surprises. It fills us with joy and excitement; it may also require us to take significant risks and to sacrifice everything.

For many congregations, a *kairos* season comes when the demographics in the church's neighborhood begin to change. For more than a hundred years, Green Meadows Presbyterian was a sleepy country church served by a series of retired ministers who preached on Sunday and cared for the sick and dying. Open fields and countless acres of pine trees surrounded their small sanctuary building. Then the suburbs of a large city began to move their way. Neighborhoods began to appear where cows had grazed. New schools were being built. A supermarket chain opened a store near the church. One day when the clerk of session was driving through the community he realized for the first time what was happening and thought about it in relation to his church. *Who are these new people?* he wondered. Then the conviction came to him: *Our church should be doing something to reach them.*

Though he may not have known the word, this man had realized that his church was in the midst of a *kairos* season. Such an opportunity for evangelism and growth had never come to this church before. If they neglected the mission field God was bringing to their door, such an opportunity might never come again. This elder had the spiritual sensitivity to recognize the opportune time, plus the courage and faith to begin urging his congregation to respond to the God-given opportunity before them. In doing so, he was exercising spiritual leadership.

QUESTIONS FOR THOUGHT AND DISCUSSION

1. Does your church have a mission statement? Can you quote all or part of it? How does it shape the life of your congregation? When was the last time it was updated?
2. Think of a time when your congregation took a significant risk. How were the leaders, pastors, and officers involved in the situation?
3. Who in your congregation knows the history of your church from its beginning well enough to make the connections between that history and the life of the congregation today? Is the history available in written form? How are new members and new pastors introduced to this history?
4. Some sessions take part of each session meeting to read and reflect on selections from Scripture, the *Book of Confessions*, or the *Book of Order* as part of their equipment for leadership. How do you think this practice would be received in your church?
5. Remember a *kairos* time in the life of your church. How did the church's leadership respond?

6

Working with Others

Jim had been a member of his small-town church for many years, but he'd suddenly stopped attending worship. One of the elders in his church, Susan, decided to pay him a visit. As they talked, Jim acknowledged that he had some negative feelings about their pastor. "When I served as chair of the stewardship drive last year, I felt that the pastor pretty much ignored our committee. He only came to the first meeting. He never seemed to want to get involved with the group, and we ended up doing our own thing without him. I felt stewardship went very well in spite of this, but I resented his unwillingness to get involved. I don't think he's a very good leader."

When Susan shared Jim's concern with Bob, their pastor, he was quite taken aback. "I never meant the committee to think I was ignoring them," he said. "They were a very talented and focused group with strong leadership. It seems to me that with a group like that, the best thing you can do is to turn them loose to do their work. They don't need anyone holding their hands or standing over them. And they did a great job. That was the best stewardship effort we have had in years and I told them so!" At the end of their conversation, Pastor Bob promised to visit Jim to try to mend the relationship. Susan and Bob both agreed that it might be helpful to have a discussion about leadership styles at the next session meeting.

The issue of a leader's style comes up frequently in churches—and in the world at large—and it's important to remember that just because you share a goal with the members of your church does not mean that it will be easy to move them toward that mutually desired goal. Your leadership style—how you function and interact with people in the process of reaching that goal—can (and often does) determine whether you get there at all. Leaders have to interact with people. A leader without followers is not a leader; he or she is simply a committee of one. Leadership involves working with people in such a way that they are able to achieve what needs to be achieved. Every leader has a different way of doing this. The particular mix of behaviors and attitudes each person uses to get the group to move toward the goal constitutes his or her leadership style.

WHAT MAKES UP A LEADERSHIP STYLE?[1]

Leadership style takes many forms, and you can find hundreds of books on the subject. The following discussion is designed to help you find your most natural leadership style. To that end I lay out some of the patterns of behavior that make up various ways of working with people. I describe these behaviors in extreme form and organize them in contrasting pairs for the sake of clarity. You will probably find your natural leadership style located somewhere between the extremes. As you read the descriptions of the behaviors, think about how you tend to behave in leadership situations and try to locate yourself.

Reactive/Proactive

"If it ain't broke, don't fix it" is the motto of reactive leaders. They wait for something to happen, and then they deal with it. Reactive leaders tend to go from one task to the next, letting things unfold naturally and reacting accordingly. They live in the present and let the most critical matter in front of them shape their agenda. Proactive leaders, in contrast, tend to want to meet the future before it comes to them. They crave long-range planning. They want to act now to shape future events instead of just letting things develop. Reactive leaders think about what needs to be done next month or next season. Proactive leaders have the next year's programs planned before the current year is half over. A reactive leader of the church's property committee will wait until a piece of equipment shows signs of wearing out and then have it replaced. A proactive leader will urge his committee to develop a five-year plan for upgrading all the equipment in the church.

Strengths of reactive leadership:

— Does not waste energy planning for things that never happen
— Usually is very aware of what the group is most interested in seeing happen at any given time
— Does not make people feel pressured to do things they can't see the need for now

Weaknesses of reactive leadership:

— Has a tendency to use short-term solutions for problems that need a long-term fix
— Can create chronic anxiety in the group by going from one crisis to the next
— In not anticipating and preventing problems, can end up spending more time, effort, and money fixing those problems when they do arise

Strengths of proactive leadership:

— Avoids a crisis mentality in the group
— Is seldom blindsided by problems that could have been avoided with foresight
— Creates energy by challenging the group with a compelling vision of the future and encouraging people to move toward it

Weaknesses of proactive leadership:

— May spend so much time planning the future that nothing is accomplished in the present
— May have little patience with people who do not want to move at the set pace
— Future-oriented plans and projects may run a higher risk of failure than those that address immediate needs

Task-Oriented/People-Oriented

The number-one priority of task-oriented leaders is to get the job done; everything else is secondary. They are highly bottom-line-oriented. Meetings led by highly task-oriented people tend to run short because little chitchat or personal interaction is allowed; the focus is doing the job. These leaders may sacrifice group process and the full involvement of group members in order to produce what they see as the best possible work product in as short a time as possible. If need be, task-oriented leaders sometimes even jettison the group entirely and do the job themselves. Because the goal is so important to them, achieving that goal is primary, and the feelings of people are less important. A task-oriented leader does not take pleasure in hurting people's feelings but is not loathe to risk doing so to achieve a goal. People who work with task-oriented leaders have the satisfaction of seeing things accomplished, but may come away feeling bruised and in some cases abused.

People-oriented leaders, in contrast, are not satisfied with an outstanding work product unless the members of the group feel good about the way it was achieved. For them, the group interaction is almost as important as the completed task. They want people to go away from a meeting feeling valued and involved. Opportunities to talk about personal interests and get to know each other better are central. Because they value good relationships so highly, people-oriented leaders may be uncomfortable with conflict in the group and may tend to avoid it instead of working through it to a productive end. In extreme cases, people-oriented leaders may even leave a job undone or partially done in order to avoid hurting someone's feelings or causing friction.

Strengths of task-oriented leadership:

—Creates energy in the group through the efficient and timely accomplishment of goals
—Keeps people focused on the importance of accomplishing something and seeing results
—Understands conflict as a positive thing that can help the group clarify its values and goals

Weaknesses of task-oriented leadership:

—Without meaning to, can hurt people deeply, even causing them to leave the group
—Groups may accomplish much, but the members can remain semi-strangers to each other
—The leadership experience can become an exercise in self-importance for the leader

Strengths of people-oriented leadership:

— Encourages group cohesion and strength
— Tends to build up individuals and promote relationships and personal growth
— Provides a healthy atmosphere for leadership development within the group

Weaknesses of people-oriented leadership:

— Runs the risk of not accomplishing much and in the process sapping energy from the group
— Avoids conflict at all costs, which can be detrimental to the long-term health of the group because issues are never settled and continue to fester
— Can encourage the evolution of groups that tend to exclude others and mainly serve to please themselves

Directive/Democratic

Leadership style also involves how a leader works with a group to make decisions. Directive leaders believe that people work best when they are told what to do, and they often believe their job is to tell the group what to do. Such leaders often are not truly happy until the group falls into line with their ideas. They place a high value on efficient and timely decision making and do not like to wait while a group mulls over a matter. Taken to an extreme, this style of leadership becomes dictatorial and autocratic. Such leaders see themselves as indispensable to the group. They know best and expect everyone else to see things their way.

Leaders who have a more democratic style want to let decisions arise from within the group. They believe the group knows best how to do its business, so they work with the group patiently until a consensus arises. For these leaders, taking charge in a directive or autocratic manner would be offensive. Extremely democratic leaders would rather the decision never be made or the task never finished than take it upon themselves to tell people what to do. Democratic leaders tend to describe themselves as facilitators or enablers. Seeing that the group is functioning well is their main job. They tend to place a low value on their own personal activity within the group. As long as the group is doing what it is supposed to do, they do not feel a need to be involved in the work at a deep level.

In certain cases, democratic leaders may withdraw from the group entirely, causing "a leadership vacuum in which group members can accomplish the task by assuming leadership roles and carrying on the work themselves."[2] The pastor in the story at the beginning of this chapter was practicing a passive variety of democratic leadership. He knew the stewardship committee had a strong chairman and creative and committed members. He made sure that the committee had access to all the resources it needed to do the job and then withdrew and let the committee members do it. His behavior, as he understood it, was a tribute to the competence and creativity of the group. If he had become totally involved with the committee, the chairman and other members would not have had space to reach their full potential.

Strengths of directive leadership:

—Allows for quick and efficient decision making
—Gives the group a sense of security; they know who is in charge
—Works best in large groups where democratic process would be slow and cumbersome

Weaknesses of directive leadership:

—Tends to make for passive followers
—The group may fall apart or be unable to function when the leader is absent
—Can cause resistance among followers who want to think for themselves

Strengths of democratic leadership:

—Strengthens group cohesion and the ability to function well together even in the leader's absence
—Decisions arrived at through group process are less vulnerable to sabotage later
—Avoids hasty or flawed decisions that reflect only the leader's knowledge and values

Weaknesses of democratic leadership:

—Can be time-consuming to work through to a group decision; group members can become bored with the process
—Leader may seem distant, passive, and uncaring, leaving group to wonder who is in charge

—The group process is susceptible to manipulation by a few strong-minded members for their own ends

Managerial/Initiative-Based

These two contrasting elements of leadership style have to do with the focus of the leader. Maintenance of a good thing is at the heart of the vision of managerial leaders. They put most of their effort into keeping the organization running smoothly in its current form. A managerial leader may begin planning for a new year by pulling out the calendar from last year and putting new dates beside last year's events. The budget for next year may be determined by adjusting the budget figures from this year slightly upward for inflation. These leaders often find their time taken up with doing what needs to be done to keep things on an even keel. When conflict arises, managerial leaders often try to work out a compromise so that everybody gets something and no one goes away angry. Sometimes, though, these leaders are surprised when, despite their hard work, the program loses energy and participation dwindles.

In contrast, leaders who function in an initiative style are always looking for the next new thing. They don't want the group to stay the way it is; they want it to become a different and better organization. These leaders enjoy change and are always on the alert for important turning points in the life of the group. For them, a new direction is a challenge and an opportunity. They believe that the best is yet to be and that the current reality is only a shadow of what the group could do in the future. They dream dreams and see visions. They like to start the budget process with a clean sheet of paper because it spurs creativity and keeps the group out of a rut. For these leaders, the best use of group time is deciding what new and different thing to do next.

This kind of leadership has also been called "transformative." It does not look at the status quo and ask how to keep things going. Instead, transformative leaders envision what could be and hold that vision out to the group to motivate change. Transformative leaders spend generous amounts of their time designing and building the new. They want people to see things in a different way. For these leaders, conflict is the natural outgrowth of change and an opportunity to bring the group together around the dream of a new future.

Strengths of managerial leadership:

— Necessary tasks are done, and people are taken care of on a day-to-day basis

— Avoids wasting time and energy in planning for the sake of planning

— Keeps group feeling secure by avoiding change and conflict

Weaknesses of managerial leadership:

— Can lead the group into extinction by avoiding necessary change

— Spends time doing what does not need to be done simply because it has always been done that way

— Group may miss exciting opportunities because it is too involved in maintenance to pursue them

— Favoring maintenance consistently over innovation tends to lead to boredom

Strengths of transformative leadership:

— Brings energy into the group through change and new possibilities

— Able to meet changing circumstances in creative ways, helping the group attain its full potential

— Stays out of ruts and avoids wasting money and time on programs that have outlived their usefulness

Weaknesses of transformative leadership:

— May be so vision-focused that day-to-day tasks and needs of people are neglected

— Creates chronic anxiety in the group when the pace of change is beyond what people can tolerate

— Prone to losing things valuable to the organization as the old is jettisoned wholesale in favor of the new

— Can lead group into exhaustion or discouragement with too ·many fruitless initiatives

THE FLEXIBLE LEADER

While most people have a style of leadership that is comfortable to them, no one set of leadership behaviors is always appropriate for every setting. For instance, a directive, highly task-oriented style of leadership could be very appropriate on the field of battle but might not work as well with a church committee. The best leaders can tailor the way they work with people to the needs of a particular situation and group. The important thing is to have the personal flexibility to choose appropriate behaviors as the situation demands. This flexibility is one of the hallmarks of good leadership.

Most people have a particular leadership style or set of behaviors with which they are most comfortable. Then they may also have a style that they naturally shift into when their primary style does not work. For instance, a mother who is very people-oriented and democratic in style may spend large amounts of time reasoning with her children, hoping that they will decide for themselves that cleaning their rooms is a good thing. After a while, however, when this strategy does not work, she may shift into a more directive mode, telling them to clean up their rooms or risk being grounded.

It is helpful to be aware of your natural leadership inclination—that is, the behaviors you naturally use in working with people without thinking about it. As we have just seen, a great variety of leadership strategies exist. Do you give orders? Do you withdraw? Do you take on more than you should? Do you try to get everyone involved? Do you go day by day, or do you keep your eyes on the future? How do you react to conflict? Do you like to give detailed instructions or let the group do its own thing? What do you want most from a leadership experience? When at first you don't succeed, what do you usually try next? Questions such as these can help you find your most natural ways of leading.

However, your natural leadership style may not be appropriate in every case. You can learn to broaden your repertoire of leadership behaviors to suit different situations, and you can practice and become more comfortable with a style of leadership that is not your natural preference. One way to do this is to observe the leadership behaviors of others when you are a member, rather than leader, of a group. Observe how the group reacts to the leader. Observe how you feel as the meeting goes on: ignored? appreciated? relaxed? tense? bored? engaged? run over? What behaviors do you observe that you would like to add to your repertoire? What does the leader do that you think is ineffective with this particular group? Observing all kinds of leaders at work and learning from them is a good way to determine how to be more flexible in your leadership style, and this flexibility will make you a more effective leader.

UNDERSTANDING YOUR GROUP

Just as leaders come in all styles, so does each group have its own personality. Understanding the character and needs of the group you are working with can give you important clues as to how to lead in that setting. Asking the questions below can help you begin to understand your particular group.

Is the group's task problem solving or policy making? The amount of long-term effect a task has on the church is a factor in choosing your leadership style. Problem-solving tasks generally involve accomplishing or deciding something on a one-time basis, such as planning an Easter egg hunt or figuring out how to run the stewardship campaign. Policy-making tasks, on the other hand, tend to have long-term effects. They involve rules that cover a wide range of situations, involve more people, and influence the future as well as the present. Establishing guidelines governing events and procedures such as weddings, funerals, building and vehicle use, the order of worship, and church staff fall into the policy-making category. They can be emotionally charged because they involve values, habits, items, people, and practices that people hold dear. Leaders can generally afford to be more directive when engaged in problem-solving tasks, especially if they are urgent. Policy-making tasks, however, often require a more participatory leadership style that aims to bring the group to buy into a shared decision.[3]

Does the group see you as a player or as the coach? Both players and coaches may exercise leadership, but it is not generally appropriate for a player to start acting like the coach. Similarly, when a team comes together for practice, they expect the coach to teach and give directions. This is the coach's role. Sports teams aren't really all that different from any other group that comes together. So, in choosing an appropriate leadership style, you need to gauge what leadership expectations your group has of you.

For instance, a highly task-focused group expects its leader to act assertively to help it do the job. This might be true, for instance, of an officer nominating committee. There is a clear task to accomplish and a deadline to meet. The group may feel under pressure to present by a certain date the names of nominees to the congregation. This kind of group wants a leader who can set out a clear process for it to follow, moves the group through that process without bogging down, and holds the group members accountable to get their work done in a timely fashion. The leader functions like the group's coach in this setting. Other groups, such as those that gather for fellowship, support, or prayer, may expect the leader to act more like a member of the group, keeping a low leadership profile, and often letting the group process evolve as it will. In this setting, the leaders may seem more like a player and less like the coach.

When you are working with a group with which you are not familiar, do not make assumptions about the expectations that group has of you. Rather, talk with others who have led that group, observe closely how the group functions, and ask questions in order to figure out the best way to lead.

Do you have the respect of the group, or do you have to earn it? Jon Clark, an elder who was also a professional bookkeeper, served for years on his church's finance committee. As time went on, he developed a directive leadership style based on his experience and knowledge in his field. When he spoke, people listened because he usually knew what he was talking about, and he knew more than anyone else. One day Jon's pastor asked him to become chair of the worship committee because the elder who was leading it had moved to take a job in another town.

Jon expected smooth sailing, given his successful prior leadership experience, but when he tried to use his usual directive style in the worship committee, he faced a major rebellion. "He doesn't know anything about music!" complained a choir member to the pastor. "What gives him the right to tell us how to do things?" fumed another committee member. "We have been working at this for years and he just walked in the door!"

This elder found out the hard way that an assertive, highly directive style works best when the group has a high degree of respect for the leader, which often takes time. Leaders who are newcomers to any group are usually best served by a more democratic, person-oriented style, which allows the group time to bond with you and learn to trust you. One exception to this general rule about newcomer-leaders occurs when a person is held in so much general esteem that her or his leadership is less likely to be questioned. A longtime beloved elder, for example, can sometimes get away with saying or doing things that would never be accepted from a young first-termer. So, what did Jon do on the worship committee to gain the members' trust? First, he made an appointment to take the choir director and the former chair of the Worship Committee out to lunch. He confessed that he felt he had started off badly with the committee, but wanted to do better. Then Jon asked them both to tell him everything they felt he needed to know about the work of the group and how it liked to operate. As they talked,

Jon took notes and asked questions that showed he really wanted to understand. Next he visited with the pastor to benefit from her understanding of the committee and its history.

Jon began the next worship committee meeting by going around the table and having each member say what part of the worship service was most important to them and why. He also spoke to the question and made it clear in his remarks that he valued worship and all the people who participated in the service each week. Jon made it a point, from that meeting on, to ask what the committee members thought about issues on the agenda before telling them what he thought should be done. He often deferred to others who had more experience in planning worship than he did, saving his more aggressive leadership behaviors for other settings. Over the next few months, the atmosphere in the worship committee thawed so that by the end of Jon's first year, he felt he had been accepted and had also learned to be comfortable with his new style of leadership.

How experienced and strong is the group? Does the group have a clear sense of its job? Has there been a history of competent leadership in the past with people feeling good about what has been accomplished? Do people have the knowledge and drive to be self-starting? Do relationships in the group seem strong and healthy? Are there other people in the group who are natural leaders? Generally speaking, the healthier and stronger a group is, the less directive the leader needs to be. If people know how to do their jobs, do them well, and seem to enjoy being together, it can be a delight to pull back and let the team do its thing.

Conversely, when the group is not functioning well, when it doesn't really have a clear grasp of what it is supposed to do, when there doesn't seem to be much energy or enjoyment in the meetings, when not much seems to be accomplished, then a more directive, assertive style can be helpful.[4] Prepare a detailed agenda in advance of the meetings. Take time to help the group sort out and look together at all the things for which the group is responsible. Let the group work on what it thinks its priorities are, and then ask each member to choose what to work on based on his or her interests and gifts. Spend time in the meetings to share and discuss information that can help the group do its tasks better. Over time, these behaviors can help weak groups become stronger and more productive.

How much follow-through do you expect of group members? The beginning of the new church school year was drawing near, and Susan, the chair of the Christian education committee, decided that the classrooms needed to be painted. The education wing had been built twenty years ago, and the church school rooms had not been painted since then. Susan looked at her calendar and the church calendar and set a painting workday for her committee. When the committee met, Susan announced that the rooms needed to be painted and that the committee would have a painting day two weeks from Saturday. No one raised any objections, and Susan urged her committee members to recruit others to help paint and then moved on to the next item on the agenda. Saturday came, and so did exactly one member of the committee.

Susan blamed the poor turnout on a lack of commitment among committee members. The real culprit, however, was probably Susan's directive, task-oriented leadership style. When a high degree of follow-through is necessary on the part of your group, a participatory style of decision making and inviting input from the members offer a better approach, especially when you're asking people to donate significant amounts of time or money toward a goal or project.

To avoid being left to paint almost alone, Susan could have worked to get her group to buy into her vision. She might have first taken them on a tour of the church school rooms. Then she might have talked with them about what they had observed and how important they felt the task of painting was. If the group came to a consensus that the rooms needed work, Susan might have asked each person to take his or her calendar out and see if the proposed date would work for them. If a significant number could come that day, Susan might then have delegated part of the work of preparation and painting to each member; if the date was problematic, the group could have decided together on a new date. She might have asked each person to be responsible for bringing some people together to help them paint a particular room or rooms. This kind of buy-in on a group decision takes work and time, but it generally pays off in a higher level of follow-through.

AVOIDING THE SLAVE AND MARTYR ROLES[5]

Along with finding an appropriate leadership style, spiritual leaders face two temptations in working with others: falling into either the slave role or the martyr role. The leader as slave takes on a disproportionately large share of the group's work while withdrawing from any effective exercise of leadership because his highest priority is to avoid conflict and keep others happy. Rather than leading the group to carry out responsibilities, the slave does it all herself. She will, for example, recruit all the ushers personally rather than delegate some of the recruiting work to other committee members. A leader acting in the slave role will drop any idea immediately if it brings about the slightest hint of disagreement. While declining to tackle difficult issues that might raise conflict or involve the group in hard decisions, a slavelike leader will occupy himself with trivial tasks so that he always seems to be very diligent.

Then there are the leaders who assume the martyr role, trying to control a group by means of guilt. The martyr takes on a disproportionate share of the group's work and then makes other members feel badly that they do not do their part. People feel sorry for the martyr and may revere him for his dedication. The martyr enjoys being pitied and likes everyone to know how indispensable he is. He may, for instance, go on vacation without leaving instructions and resources for the group in his absence. If things fall apart while he's gone, he sees this as evidence that the group is totally dependent on him. He lets the group know that their dependence is his cross, and he must bear it. The martyr's message to the group is, "You can't do anything without me."

Leaders acting out of either the slave or the martyr role seldom praise and often criticize. Communication in groups they lead is often poor. Both slaves and martyrs do far more than their share of the work, not because the group needs them to do so, but because doing it makes them feel good. The sad thing is that these leaders tend to create followers who are passive and unengaged in the work of the group. These unhealthy leadership patterns deprive groups and individuals of opportunities to meet challenges and achieve success. The growth of the group is stunted because of the leader's behavior, which is certainly not effective leadership.

SERVING OUR SERVANT LORD

Politicians sometimes refer to themselves as "servants of the people," by which they mean that they are elected by the people to further their welfare and that they serve at the pleasure of those who elected them. Leaders in the church are also servants, but we are first and foremost servants of Christ. He is the one who called us into the church. He is the one who called us into leadership through the voice of his people, and it is to Christ that we will ultimately give an accounting of our leadership.

Therefore, your number-one priority as a church officer must be to seek and do his will. One of the most challenging responsibilities of leadership is convincing God's people to go where they may not want to go, at least not at first. The truth is that often what people need the most, they want the least. Keeping your ultimate loyalty fixed on Jesus frees you from the tyranny of congregational opinion and enables you to continue to lead when trouble and conflict arise.

As a spiritual leader in the church, you should remember that the authority you have been given is a trust from God. It comes from Christ, the Lord and head of the church, and is to be used for the good of his people and the advancement of his kingdom. Jesus once asked Peter, "Do you love me?" In reply to Peter's "yes," Jesus said, "Feed my sheep" (John 21:17). Good leaders must be diligent about nurturing the Lord's sheep and protecting the welfare of the flock even at significant expense to themselves, which means that you must keep a close eye on your own motivations. Ask yourself: Am I working for the group's good or for my own? Am I most concerned about helping the group grow and be productive, or am I more concerned about getting my own way or taking it easy? Am I truly committed to leading the group to seek God's will, no matter what it turns out to be? Questions like these keep us honest, and spiritual leaders should develop and practice the discipline of reflecting self-critically on them regularly.

As you consider how you should exercise leadership, remember that the high-water mark of spiritual leadership was Jesus taking a towel and a basin and beginning to wash and dry his disciples' feet. Some people have suggested that, being in a borrowed room, no servants were available to take on this menial task, and no disciple was willing to humble himself to do the work of a servant. Yes, Jesus could have given the disciples a lecture on humility and then ordered them to wash each other's feet. Instead, he took up the tools of the servant and did it himself, in love, showing them how they were to treat each other. This ideal of servant leadership has challenged Christians ever since. It is much easier to trade the lowly towel for more impressive instruments of power. However, as we choose how to lead in the church, the most crucial thing to remember is that we belong to Jesus Christ, who came among us "as one who serves" (Luke 22:27).

QUESTIONS FOR THOUGHT AND DISCUSSION

1. Reflect on the pairs of contrasting behaviors that make up the leadership styles described in this chapter. For each pair, decide which is your most natural leadership behavior.

2. What are the positive and negative results you have experienced in using your most natural style of working with people?

3. Is there a particular leadership style that your congregation seems to expect from its pastor(s) and officers? If so, why do you think this style is preferred?

4. Have you ever observed a servant leader at work? How did people react to this leader?

5. What is the difference between a servant leader and leaders who act like slaves or martyrs as described in this chapter?

7

The Church:
Christ's Body in Our World

Few things are more rewarding than being a part of a wonderful church. Many of us initially agree to be leaders in our congregations because we have had this experience and want to give back by serving the church that has given us so much. We begin the experience of being officers with great expectation, but then we sometimes find ourselves confronted with what seems like the dark, underside of the church, filled with conflict, criticism, and problems to be solved. So it is that new and idealistic church officers, eventually—sometimes far too quickly—are forced to confront the reality that most if not all human vices and sins can be found in some form or another in the church and its members. This realization can be very disheartening, and as the ideals these officers have brought to the job crumble under the weight of reality, some grow disillusioned and even fall away from the church altogether, which is why spiritual leaders need to have a true under-standing of the unique nature of the church as they do their work.

No other organization on the face of the earth is exactly like the church of Jesus Christ. The key doctrine for understanding it is the incar-nation. Christians believe that the eternal God who created the universe and everything in it was born onto this earth as a human baby. The baby's name was Jesus. The early church struggled for centuries to understand exactly who Jesus was, finally expressing its conclusions in AD 381 in what we know as the Nicene Creed. In it they declared that Jesus was "true God from true God, begotten, not made, of one Being with the

Father," yet they say he also "became truly human."[1] The great paradox of the incarnation is that Jesus was both 100 percent divine and 100 percent human, all at the same time.

The church also is both divine and human. As a divine, God-ordained institution, it is holy because it is created and used by God. In the church, Scripture is proclaimed and the sacraments are given as God's gifts to human beings. Jesus Christ promises to make himself known in the world through the church. It is very important to realize that God, not human beings, created the church. Our Form of Government early on states that "Christ calls the Church into being, giving it all that is necessary for its mission to the world, for its building up, and for its service to God" (G-1.0100b). Theologian Shirley Guthrie continues to draw out this idea by saying, "The church, therefore, is not like a club or fraternity or group of like-minded people who enjoy each other's company, form an organization for their mutual benefit and enjoyment, and set up the constitution and rules of membership to suit themselves."[2] The church is a supernatural, divine community through which we receive salvation and eternal life.

Keep this in mind, because the church's divine nature is not always easy to see. Sometimes it takes great faith to believe that the church as we know it is the body of Christ. But the truth is that the church was never intended to be a group of holy people who are in themselves morally superior to everyone else. Remember that the apostle Peter, the rock on whom Jesus said he would build his church, denied his Lord three times, yet Jesus forgave Peter and commissioned him to "feed my sheep" (John 21:15–17). Early in the church's history, believers and even some priests denied the faith under threat of torture or death. When the persecution passed, these folks often wanted to come back into the fold, and the church had to decide whether to allow them back and also whether sacraments were valid if performed by a priest who had once denied Christ. The church concluded that no repentant sinner could be barred from the body of Christ, and also that the validity of the sacraments did not depend on the sinlessness of the clergy performing them. From its very beginning, the church has been a community of sinners daily seeking forgiveness and new life through Jesus Christ.

Although the Apostles' Creed speaks of "the holy catholic Church," that holiness does not reside in the individual members. Rather, as Guthrie notes, "The body is holy only because the Head is *the* 'Holy One.' Holiness is not found in the church and its membership as such, but in him from whom they seek forgiveness, change, help, and new direction. When asked about the holiness of the church, Christians . . . can only point to his goodness, strength, purity, and wisdom."[3] This way of being church makes us radically dependent on the grace of Christ in order to be the body of Christ. We cannot do it with human strength, human goodness, or good intentions.

The apostle Paul goes so far as to say that the very human frailty and imperfection of the church serves to glorify God: "We have this treasure in clay jars [KJV: earthen vessels], so that it may be made clear that this extraordinary power belongs to God and does not come from us" (2 Cor. 4:7). There *is* a divine treasure in the church, but it is contained in the earthen vessel of human frailty and imperfection. Paul says the reason for commingling of the divine and the earthen is that when good things happen in and through the church, it will be obvious to everyone that they must come from God because earthen vessels cannot produce such results.

But having said all of this, the point is not that Christians should stop trying to be godly. Rather, the church *is* the body of Christ; our job is, by the grace and Spirit of God, to live into this reality. Our *Book of Order* states, "The Church is called to be a sign in and for the world of the new reality which God has made available to people in Jesus Christ. . . . The Church is the body of Christ, both in its corporate life · and in the lives of its individual members, and is called to give shape and substance to this truth" (G-3.0200a, c). When people want to see what the will of God is for human life and community, they should be able to see it reflected in the lives of Christians and especially in the communal life of the church.

Scripture does not say, "Someday you will be the body of Christ," or "If you try hard, you might get to be the body of Christ," or "If you reach certain levels of perfection, you could be the body of Christ." The statement is absolute: "Now you are the body of Christ and individually members of it" (1 Cor. 12:27). Yet the church is also a human institution full of all the weaknesses and sins to be found in humanity, and spiritual leaders must work within this tension. The challenge facing all Christians, and especially leaders, is to hold on to the truth of the church's divine nature while at the same time not becoming discouraged by its human weaknesses. Those who manage this best are those who let the church's imperfections drive them to their knees in prayer before the one who gave his life to create the church and promises to perfect it in the end.

SEEING DIFFICULTIES AS CONTAINING
GOD-GIVEN OPPORTUNITIES

WANTED: Church officers to serve a three-year term. Duties involve long hours spent doing the work of the church and lots of meetings. May end up skipping meals, losing sleep, and sacrificing family time. Position may entail conflict and knowing things you would really rather not know. Must be willing to make hard decisions on a regular basis. May be required to work closely with people who may drive you crazy. In return for the above, you will have to deal with the criticism and discontent of others. Must have own spiritual resources. Only the prayerful need apply.

This tongue-in-cheek job description points out the potential difficulties of being a church officer. Few officers complete a term of service without encountering at least one of these situations. Yes, many rewards go along with serving God in church leadership, and naturally, nominating committees tend to focus on them when recruiting candidates to serve. So it can come as a shock to first-time officers when the difficulties of the work present themselves.

Even the most effective spiritual leaders cannot avoid problems and obstacles. They are part of the human package, even in the church. However, the best church officers learn to let problems be their teachers. As the saying goes, when the church hands them lemons, they learn to make lemonade. A large measure of their success lies in the fact that they have the theological tools necessary to think about how God might be at work in the difficulties they face. Three biblical principles are especially important to understanding and dealing with difficult situations, and they can help you grow as a leader in the midst of the struggles of leadership: (1) God can bring good out of any situation; (2) God uses our weaknesses; and (3) God leads, we follow.

God Can Bring Good out of Any Situation

Romans 8:28 states: "We know that all things work together for good for those who love God, who are called according to his purpose." Christians have used this Scripture since the early days of the faith to find comfort and hope when things go wrong. This text has also been translated "We know that all things work together for good" (KJV) or "In all things God works for the good" (NIV). Whichever translation you choose, the central thrust of the passage is one of hope and redemption. There is no situation from which the grace of God is excluded. God is always at work to mine good out of the dross of our disaster and disappointments.

Another way to say this is that God never wastes anything. God can use even our sins, mistakes, and tragedies to further God's purposes for us and for God's kingdom. Many churches have put this truth to work in the area of pastoral care through the Stephen Ministry program, which links those who have gone through a painful situation (divorce, grief, illness, etc.) with those who are currently going through it. Stephen Ministers draw on their experience of pain to help another. In this way they allow God to use the dark side of their lives to produce good. God can use anything we put in God's hands to further God's purposes.

Living into the truth that God can work in all things for good helps church leaders maintain a healthy and humble hope. That hope is not based on how skilled, competent, or holy we are. Rather it takes into account that we are all human beings who fail regularly in spite of our best intentions, and in addition to dealing with our own failures and sins, church leaders must also deal with the sins and mistakes of others. To say that God works for good in all things is to say that nothing can keep God's will from being done in and among us. God is stronger than anything that can come at us. To believe in God's sovereignty is to put no boundaries on God's ability to use whatever life sends our way to further God's purposes.

The most bitter disappointment and the sharpest grief can actually open the door for God to do great things. Scripture shows us that God does God's best work under the most dire circumstances and at times when everything seems lost. Recall the prophet Ezekiel, who stands looking at a valley full of human bones, "and they were very dry" (Ezek. 37:2). God says to him that "these bones are the whole house of Israel. They say, 'Our bones are dried up, and our hope is lost; we are cut off completely'" (Ezek. 37:11). The Spirit of God blows across the dead dry bones and they stand "on their feet, a vast multitude" (Ezek. 37:10). Other examples include the many barren, hopeless women in Scripture who gave birth through God's intervention, and whose children grew up to do important things for God (Gen. 18:1–15; 21:1–7; 1 Sam. 1:1–28; Luke 1:1–25). The potential disaster of a hungry crowd in a deserted place with no food opened the door for Jesus to do one of his great miracles, the feeding of the five thousand. And when all seemed lost and the stone was rolled across the opening to Jesus' grave, God had the last word over evil in raising him from the dead. The Bible is full of stories like these, which show that when God is involved, there are no hopeless situations.

Spiritual leaders who understand this principle treat trials and roadblocks as paths to God's future instead of dead ends. One Christmas eve in the 1950s, Hemphill Memorial Presbyterian Church faced just such a potential dead end when its sanctuary burned to the ground. The fire was so traumatic that, even decades later when I became their pastor, members still talked about the trauma. This beloved classic country church building had held decades of memories for the congregation and the community. The situation was even more discouraging because the church's membership had been shrinking for years. Some folks thought the fire would be the end of the church, yet this congregation was blessed with visionary leaders who were able to look beyond the disaster of the moment to see the possibilities of a new future. The decision was made to build a new sanctuary of contemporary design where the old one had stood, and as these plans went forward, the church started to revive. Its new life and energy attracted others, and for the first time in years, the church grew. The key factor in this positive outcome was the leadership of church officers who believed that God could bring new life out of the ashes and work in all things for good.

God Can Use Our Weaknesses

When we think of offering ourselves to God for service in the church, most of us think of offering God our strengths. We hardly ever think of offering God our weaknesses and our lacks. But remember the apostle Paul, who had what he called a thorn in the flesh, some kind of weakness or problem that he believed was hampering him in doing God's work. Three times he prayed for this thing to be taken away from him. God's answer was, "My grace is sufficient for you, for [my] power is made perfect in weakness" (2 Cor. 12:9).

God can use our weaknesses as well as our strengths. In fact, sometimes our weaknesses can glorify God more than our strengths. Look at it this way: When we operate out of our strengths, the focus is on us. We are in control, and it's easy to slip into thinking that we are doing it all ourselves. We're not leaving room for God to do much. But when we operate out of our weakness, we leave God plenty of room to work. We are much more aware of God's power enabling us to do what we could never do by ourselves. The focus is on God much more than on us.

Personal weaknesses can come into sharp focus in church leadership, especially in working with difficult people. It is a fortunate officer who can get through a full term of service without having to deal with someone who is a trial. Jesus commanded us to "love one another as I have loved you " (John 15:12), but you may find yourself dealing with people you have a hard time tolerating, let alone loving. It is easy to avoid confessing your weakness by deciding and acting on the idea that some people are just completely unlovable. The word Jesus uses to tell us to love one another is the Greek word *agapē*. *Agapē* is not romantic love; it basically means loving what is not in itself lovely or attractive. Jesus is telling us to love those who are unlovely just as God loved us when we ourselves were lost in sin. We know that the only way we will ever be able to deal in a positive way with difficult people is if God enables us to do it. When we pray that God will help us to be graceful toward them, we are offering God our weakness and asking that God's power may be made perfect through our thorn in the flesh.

We are similarly encouraged to put our weaknesses in God's hands when we are asked to do something for which we have no talent. Maybe your gifts lie in the area of church property management, but your church is desperately in need of people to staff the nursery. Or you're called on to lead a committee when you've never led one in your life. Or you're almost paralyzed with fear when you have to say anything in front of your small Sunday school class, but then you are called on to speak in front of the congregation. Given your weaknesses, these things may seem like invitations to embarrassment and failure, yet the God whose power is made perfect in our weakness can redeem such situations. God can give us what we need to do the job, and God uses these experiences of weakness to teach us deeper truths. We may be humbled; we may be reminded in painful ways that we are not perfect, yet these are opportunities for spiritual growth as we put ourselves in God's hands and let God do what God wants to do. If we always live only out of our strengths, we will never know the fullness of Christ's power dwelling in us.

When Jesus took the five loaves and two fish into his hands, he did not think about what a pittance it was to feed such a great crowd. Instead he focused on the power of God, and look what happened: he blessed and broke the bread and the story says that it was enough. Effective spiritual leaders likewise are able to see weakness and lack as an invitation for God to do great things in them and in the church.

God Leads and We Follow

My husband and I took dancing lessons once. I wanted to learn all those marvelous dances that you see in the old movies. My dreams hit a major snag, however, when both of us kept trying to lead. We stepped all over each other's feet, and the dancing lessons never got us anywhere. Leading and following are just as important in things spiritual as they are in dancing. God is to do the leading, and we are to do the following. Often, however, we do the leading and expect God to follow us. During the Civil War, someone asked Abraham Lincoln if he thought God was on the side of the Union. Lincoln replied that he hoped the Union was on the side of God. Often in the church we decide what to do on our own and then pray that God will be on our side and bless it. We are leading and expecting God to follow.

Sometimes it takes a failure to make us realize that we have put the cart before the horse. A minister I know was asked to lead a Lenten retreat at a friend's church. He accepted the invitation eagerly and confidently. He chose some of his best sermons and most inspiring talks. In due time he packed his bags and went to take the gospel to this other congregation. About halfway through his first sermon, he realized that he was not getting through. The congregation seemed listless and half-asleep, and so it went for the rest of the weekend. No matter how lively and engaging he tried to be, nothing seemed to click with these people. He left embarrassed, feeling like a failure. Some time later he realized that he had not prayed at all about the weekend. He had accepted the invitation, chosen the topics, planned the messages, and gone about the weekend confidently, expecting God to follow along. The problem was that he hadn't invited the Holy Spirit, who could have caused the sparks of the gospel to catch fire among the people, to partner with him in leading the weekend.

The temptation to take the reins out of God's hands and put them into our own is very strong and seems to be part of human nature. Failures can become blessings if they teach us that in everything that goes on in the church and in our individual ministries, God leads and we are to follow. Few spiritual truths are more central to effective spiritual leadership than this.

CONFLICT HAPPENS

Someone can be a minimally active member of a congregation and never come into contact with conflict in the church. She or he may come to worship regularly, attend Sunday school, and be a member of a women's circle or men's group, but be oblivious to any discord within the body.

But church officers come to know the church at a deeper level, and this knowledge includes knowledge about friction, disagreement, and even dislike between people. This vantage point can be disillusioning for elders who have very high ideals for the church, but one must remember that conflict is a natural part of human interaction; where there are human beings, there will be conflict. Effective spiritual leaders are not surprised by conflict. They expect it and prepare themselves to deal with it in healthy ways.

The bigger question is how to prepare yourself for something you know you'd rather not do. Theology can provide some assistance, and one helpful piece of theological equipment to use in understanding and grappling with conflict is the process of sanctification, which refers to the process of God working in us to make us more godly, more like Jesus. When we claim God's grace for our salvation, we are also at the same time claiming God's grace for becoming godly people. The Holy Spirit, having brought us to the point of accepting God's gift of salvation, then goes to work to make us godly. The key word here is "process." Sanctification is an ongoing enterprise that lasts a lifetime and will not be complete until we stand before God in heaven. Since we are all in process as Christians, our behavior at church and in all of life is a mixture of the good and the not so good. We are a people under construction. We are sinners and saints at the same time, and the Holy Spirit isn't finished with us yet. Thus, conflict is a normal and, if understood and well managed, even beneficial part of church life, one that allows us to clarify our priorities and may even produce better ideas.

Sometimes friction in the church is about a clear issue or problem to be solved, such as whether smoking on the church grounds should be allowed, or who is allowed to be married in the church sanctuary. When this is the case, people of goodwill can usually come together and find a mutually agreeable solution. Healthy organizations recognize and name problems before the atmosphere around them becomes too emotional or personalized, and strategies such as compromise, collaboration, and negotiation are implemented to help the group work on the solution. When this happens, all parties go away with an answer to the problem that they can live with, and they may even feel proud of how the group reached the answer.

Much of the conflict in churches, however, has to do not with resolvable issues but with how human beings relate to each other.

Church conflict is far more often about people's desires and needs than about theological principles or substantive points of doctrine. Dealing with personalities and feelings can be emotional and illogical, which can be scary stuff, especially for people who are used to functioning mainly as logical problem solvers in their life outside the church.

In chapter 8 I try to help you deal with the realities of conflict between people. The approach I use is called family systems theory, and it can be helpful both inside and outside the church. Remember that conflict is part of normal human interaction and nothing to be ashamed of, in the church or elsewhere. The important thing is to deal with conflict in ways that bring glory to God and add to the health of the church and its effectiveness for mission.

QUESTIONS FOR THOUGHT AND DISCUSSION

1. How have you experienced the church being the body of Christ, a holy community?
2. How have you experienced the tension between the church as body of Christ and the church as an all-too-human institution?
3. Have you seen God bring good out of a situation that on its face seemed negative?
4. In your experience, what causes conflict in the church? How can leaders work to keep conflict from getting out of hand?
5. "A church that never experiences conflict is a dead church." How do you react to this statement?

8

Understanding the Church as an Emotional System

Relationships bring us much of what is good in life. Family relationships helped mold us into the people we are. Much of what we learned about how to navigate through this world we learned in relationship with parents, friends, teachers, and mentors. We lean on our relationships with fellow church members in times of trouble, sickness, and death. At the deepest level of existence, our relationship with God gives us abundant life. When Christians declare that God is a Trinity, we are saying that relationship is at the heart of who God is. Relationships are great things. Sometimes, however, they bring us pain or involve us in conflict.

The church is first and foremost a system of relationships. Some of the challenges that spiritual leaders in the church face come from dealing with fellow church members and church staff. "What most unites all spiritual leaders," rabbi and psychologist Edwin Friedman has observed, "is not a set of beliefs or practices but the factors that contribute to our stress."[1] These factors often involve other people and, hence, relationships. If negotiating one-on-one relationships can be stressful, the pressures only multiply when you find yourself negotiating a whole church full of relationships. Such is the setting in which spiritual leaders do their work.

John, the clerk of session, arrived at First Presbyterian one Sunday morning to find Mary, a member of the worship committee, in tears. "I'm leaving the church," she said. "I never want to see that man again!"

"That man" was Richard, the choir director, who had asked Mary to move the two arrangements of memorial flowers off their accustomed pedestals in front of the choir and to put them somewhere else. The flowers had a strong scent that some choir members found unpleasant and set off some allergies. Mary explained that the flowers had been given in memory of a parishioner, whose family had asked Mary to ensure that they were placed in the sanctuary. The family was coming to church that very day and would expect to see them in a place of honor on the platform. Richard had insisted, Mary told John, that the flowers could not stay where they were. She continued to complain, telling John about a number of other things Richard had done to make her job on the worship committee difficult. No one ever listened to her, she complained, and the pastor always took Richard's side.

Deciding there was a problem here to be solved, John went into the sanctuary to talk with Richard. He found another angry person who was eager to vent. "No one appreciates how important the choir is to this congregation! We knock ourselves out week after week to provide music for the service, and they don't even care enough to move the smelly flowers out from under our noses." Richard went on to tell John how hurt he was when the worship committee did not approve a salary increase for him in this year's budget. "And not only that," he said, "but I found out about it through an e-mail from the pastor! He didn't even bother to tell me face to face." When John left the sanctuary some time later, the flowers were still sitting on the pedestals in front of the choir loft.

John just experienced firsthand the church as a system, where every part is related to and affects every other part. Churches are organisms like a human body. You cannot understand the body by looking only at the foot or the elbow. As the apostle Paul pointed out, "If one member suffers, all suffer together with it; if one member is honored, all rejoice together with it" (1 Cor. 12:26).

A church's individual members, pastors, staff members, and others—such as former members or pastors—jointly create something that is much more than the sum of that church's parts. When an incident happens in one area of the church—the choir, for instance—it vibrates outward to touch every other part. In the church, nothing is ever as simple as it looks. You can understand why things happen as they do in a church only by understanding how the system operates as a whole, not by looking at the individual persons or incidents. John's conversations with Mary and Richard revealed a tangle of disrupted relationships involving not only the two of them, but also the pastor, choir, worship committee, and others throughout the church.

In addition to being a body or physical system, the church is also an emotional system. Church members do not check their joy, anger, frustration, happiness, sadness, or anxiety at the door. When people come to church, they bring all their emotions and emotional needs with them and, often unconsciously, act them out there. They bring all their family habits (healthy or otherwise) into their church family. They bring their own level of personal maturity or immaturity. All of these come into play in every area of the church's life.

To say the church is an emotional system is to say that the church has an emotional climate. You can walk into some churches and tell almost immediately that they are moving forward, warm, and alive. Other churches give off a sense of sadness, tension, or even death. I came to realize that an entire congregation could be depressed when three honored and beloved members of my congregation died in the same month. They were pillars of that church, and when they were removed, the whole congregation was shaken. Even members who were not personally close to them felt the effect their loss had on the system. As a result, the spiritual leaders in the church had to deal with not just the sorrow of our church's individual members but a general depression in the church's emotional system.

An important factor in the health or sickness of a church is how well its leaders function within its emotional system: how do they react when the church is experiencing transition or threat and feeling a high level of anxiety? More than anything else, anxiety seems to be at the root of much of the trouble that happens in congregations. The rest of this chapter offers tools to deal with congregational life that come out of a psychological school of thought called family systems theory. This way of understanding the church grew out of the work of Rabbi Edwin Friedman. In the 1980s he served a synagogue congregation while at the same time conducting a practice in marriage and family counseling. Friedman noted over time that some of the same dynamics present in troubled families were also present in troubled synagogues and churches, and many of the practices that helped families get better also worked in synagogues and churches. His wisdom can help spiritual leaders deal with tensions in the church in healthy and productive ways.

ANXIETY AS A RESPONSE TO CHANGE

Anxiety can strike any church at any time. It can be caused by a specific event, such as the retirement of a beloved pastor or a demographic change in the community. People begin to wonder, "What will become of us?" The death of an important church member can create anxiety as people live into the vacuum caused by that person's loss. A conflict between influential members or between members and the pastor can create an atmosphere of nervousness and worry. Anything that causes people to feel threatened, anything that upsets the status quo, can make for anxiety in the church.

Anxiety can also be a chronic presence in a church. Like a case of rheumatism, it never really goes away and can flare up and be debilitating. When important issues or conflicts in the congregation's life are repeatedly ignored or smoothed over, anxiety grows over time as people wait for the next eruption. Or a church loses its mission and has no focus or clear goals, and its members feel anxiety and fall into conflict with each other—because they have nothing better to do. Sometimes people are anxious because they share a general feeling that certain needs are not being met and the church is in decline; they wonder whether the church they love will survive or not.

Ironically, chronically anxious churches tend to approach life conservatively, avoiding risks and having little energy for the innovative, the result being little opportunity to replace anxiety with hope. It is hard to do new things and break new ground when you are constantly circling the wagons against a perceived threat. Conflict and loss of membership are often characteristics of such churches, because when people are threatened, their fight-or-flight responses come into play.

Anxiety is a normal human response to very real threats we face every day. A far larger problem than anxiety itself—whether anxiety in the church or personal anxiety—is the failure to recognize or resolve anxiety, and when either of those situations occurs, people can act in ways that can hurt the whole church. In the situation mentioned earlier, Richard the choir director at First Presbyterian was anxious about his job, fearing that he was unappreciated and about to be let go by the church. Mary came to church after a vicious fight with her teenage son, who accused her of being a bad mother and called her worthless. Neither Mary nor Richard was aware that they were bringing dynamite into the church that morning, but their anxieties kept them from addressing the problem of the heavily scented flowers in a way that was both logical and mutually respectful. And it may not end with them. Just as throwing a rock into a pond causes ripples, so Richard's and Mary's anxiety may move out into the rest of the congregation.

TOO MUCH TOGETHERNESS

Human beings function best when there is a balance in their life between intimacy and distance. The need to feel close to other human beings is part of human nature. Infants who are not touched, held, and talked to do not develop properly. People tend to feel lonely and depressed when they do not have enough togetherness in their lives. At the same time, however, most people benefit from a certain amount of healthy distance in their relationships with others. When people are too emotionally attached to other people, they tend to react very strongly to whatever others say or do, and this reaction can make things worse. For instance, in some married couples if the wife becomes depressed, the husband also becomes depressed, so instead of his being an encouraging presence for her, they both spiral down into depression together. Or if the husband gets angry, even though what he is angry about has nothing to do with her, the wife reacts by becoming irritable and defensive. Healthy distance means that each person has enough self-possession to be calm and helpful even when the other is angry, anxious, or depressed.

These same dynamics come into play in church life as they do in the family. A church with too much togetherness can be a very tense place. If one person is upset, the whole church can get upset, and when people are unhappy, their leaders can easily become anxious. Since in most churches somebody is unhappy most of the time, being such a leader can be very stressful. How do leaders attempt to cope with this stress?

Some church officers try to cope by distancing themselves from other members. They stop attending meetings regularly. They slip into worship services late and leave during the last hymn. Or they may distance themselves emotionally in ways that cut off the rest of the congregation, becoming irritable and unapproachable when they are at church.

Sometimes people deal with too much togetherness by leaving the church altogether, as happened with the clerks of session I mentioned in the introduction to this book. Functioning as lightning rods in an emotionally charged system burned them out. The only way they could get some healthy distance, some room to breathe, was to leave.

Another strategy for dealing with anxious and critical people is by overfunctioning—taking responsibility for tasks others should be doing.[2] Here's an example: the grounds chairman goes out late Saturday afternoon to cut the church lawn when the person who has been assigned this job hasn't done it or hasn't done it to the chairman's specifications. The chairman mows the lawn so that he does not have to confront directly the person who was supposed to do it and so he doesn't have to listen to members complain the next day about how bad the lawn looks. But he resents the action he took, and he goes to church the next day feeling put upon and burdened. This kind of behavior is not good for the person or for the church, and it can have a number of bad results.

For instance, overfunctioning leaders can create passive, underfunctioning followers. The Christian education committee chair does all the recruiting of church school teachers herself rather than asking the rest of the committee to help. She ends up feeling resentful, which affects her recruiting negatively because people sense her irritation and a lack of enthusiasm, and so they are slow to respond. Moreover, she's teaching her committee that recruiting is the chair's responsibility, not theirs, and so the situation will never change. The leader's willingness to do too much enables others to feel comfortable doing too little. Overfunctioning also creates a leadership vacuum in the group since no one is working with the leader to learn how to get things done.

Further, a person can experience spiritual fallout from doing too much. Rabbi Friedman notes that "one of the subtlest yet most fundamental effects of overfunctioning is spiritual. It destroys the spiritual quality of the overfunctioner."[3] The joy and blessing that can come from serving God are sapped out of church work when it is done out of anxiety or the feeling that "I have to do it or it won't get done." It becomes a heavy burden and sooner or later will wear people out. They may lose their sense of relationship with God altogether, and only a lifeless sense of duty keeps them going. Chairs of committees, clerks of session, Presbyterian Women officers, pastors, and church staff members are all at high risk for the spiritual fallout of overfunctioning.

TRIANGLING

Another way people deal with anxiety is by creating an emotional triangle. When two people or groups of people feel uncomfortable with each other and don't want to confront a problem directly, they will often triangle, or bring in a third party to help them feel better. Remember Mary and Richard and the flowers? They were trying to triangle John into their conflict. By putting him in the middle of their fight, they were trying to avoid dealing with each other. Whenever a person becomes emotionally involved with what is essentially someone else's issue, a triangle is probably in the making.

For instance, when the pastor who feels underpaid complains to the church secretary about how unappreciative and stingy the congregation is, the pastor is triangling the secretary into what is essentially a matter she needs to resolve with the session. Venting to the secretary is easier than confronting the session with her desire for a raise. By complaining to the secretary, the pastor elevates the secretary to the status of a peer. The secretary may feel honored to be the one the pastor talks to about her dissatisfaction and may encourage more of it. On the pastor's side, this "it's us against the congregation" venting may provide enough emotional relief that the pastor never gets up the courage to ask the session for a raise.

Being triangled is an occupational hazard for church officers. Maria Jimenez, a deacon, visits Mrs. Sinclair, who is homebound. Mrs. Sinclair complains to Maria that the pastor does not come to see her as often as she feels he should. She talks about how frustrated she is with the pastor's sermons, which she listens to on tape, and bemoans the fact that "this new pastor is not half the man our last pastor was." Maria asks Mrs. Sinclair if she has ever voiced her concerns to the pastor personally, but the elderly woman is shocked and says she would never think of such a thing. Instead she continues to pour criticism into the ears of the deacon for the next half hour. This member-pastor-officer triangle happens so frequently in the church that some officers think part of their job is to get into the middle of it. They become reservoirs of criticism from the congregation about the pastors or other staff, with the unfortunate result that pastors and unhappy parishioners never confront each other directly. In situations like this, problems are rarely resolved, and relationships tend over time to deteriorate.

In the case above, Maria left the visit resolving to pray for guidance about the problem of Mrs. Sinclair's negative relationship with the new pastor. After doing so, two weeks later she made an appointment to talk with the pastor. In her conversation with him, she focused not on Mrs. Sinclair's specific grievances but rather on her close relationship with the last pastor and what Maria felt to be her need now to feel connected with the new pastor. The pastor responded by promising to visit Mrs.

Sinclair and to try to get to know her better. Maria warned him to be prepared for a possible chilly reception at first, but they both agreed that it was worth the effort to reach out to a lonely homebound member in this way. As it turned out, Mrs. Sinclair received the pastor's visit with guarded warmth. Over time they developed such a positive relationship that Mrs. Sinclair told him she wanted him to do her funeral with the former pastor assisting.

In working in this situation to bring Mrs. Sinclair and the pastor together, Maria was working as a true peacemaker. If the relationship between the pastor and Mrs. Sinclair had remained negative in spite of Maria's efforts, she must still avoid being triangled into the middle of Mrs. Sinclair's negativity. The best approach in such a situation is to have the people involved work out their problems together. However, if those efforts do not succeed, Maria should set a firm boundary around this subject and not allow Mrs. Sinclair to use her as a dumping ground for her criticism of the pastor. She can say something like, "Mrs. Sinclair, I really enjoy visiting with you, but I am going to have to ask you not to share your criticisms of the pastor with me. It doesn't do either one of us really any good. I am happy to talk with you about anything but that."

IMPORTANCE OF A NONANXIOUS PRESENCE

Picture Jesus sleeping through a raging storm in the bottom of the boat while his terrified disciples work to keep the boat from sinking (Mark 4:35–41). Jesus was able to stay calm in the middle of others' anxiety. Rabbi Friedman called this ability being a nonanxious presence. One of the very best things a leader can do for a group immersed in anxiety and trouble is to be a nonanxious presence. The behavior of a church's spiritual leaders is a key factor in determining how that church deals with anxiety and crisis. If leaders can create an atmosphere of calm about a situation, people can often solve the problems themselves.[4]

This kind of calm is crucial in organizations, because when people become highly anxious, their ability to solve problems logically decreases dramatically. Their interactions devolve to the level of personalities, and conflicts become intractable. It will make a great deal of difference, for instance, how the clerk of session John responds to his encounters with Mary and Richard. If he approaches the situation with low anxiety and a sense of humor, urging them to work out their differences for the good of the church, the impact of this conflict on the congregation will be lessened. However, if John, a key leader, allows himself to assume Mary and Richard's anxiety and starts spreading it through the church, a messy conflict may be on the way.

For the healing balm of nonanxious presence to do its work in the church, leaders must stay calm while also staying closely in touch with others in the congregation. It will not help if the pastor hides in the office or the elders drop out of sight. When, in the midst of church turbulence, people can't see their officers, they might begin to wonder if anyone is in charge. But when a church's leaders are actively present in the congregation during hard times, calmly trying to understand people, showing genuine concern, praying with people, approaching matters objectively, and maintaining a sense of humor, chances are the church will be able to deal constructively with whatever is plaguing it.

Developing this level of calm is, in part at least, a spiritual work. In order to be a nonanxious presence, we need to have one in our own lives. The ultimate source of spiritual peace is faith in a faithful God. Jesus did not need to go into a panic during the storm because he knew that his Abba (father) had the situation under control. A well-nourished relationship with God and a sense that God is faithful gives leaders something to stand on in a crisis.

HEALTHY LEADERS, HEALTHY CHURCH

How can you as a leader help your church become healthier? One way is through working on what Rabbi Friedman calls self-differentiation. Self-differentiation means that you have an identity and an emotional life apart from the group. You are not totally swallowed by what is going on in the congregation. You have some healthy distance and can see things objectively. You are able to avoid becoming all caught up in the church's emotional upheavals to the point where the rest of your life is affected and you cannot function effectively. There is payoff for the church, too, as Friedman noted: "If a leader will take primary responsibility for his or her own position as 'head' and work to define his or her own goals and self, *while staying in touch* with the rest of the organism [church], there is more than a reasonable chance that the body may follow. There may be initial resistance but, if the leader can stay in touch with the resisters, the body will usually go along."[5]

One pastor realized that she was making strides toward differentiation when she refused to allow an anxious church member to spoil her

Easter. Arriving at church early on Easter morning, full of joy and eager for celebration, the pastor found a mean-spirited letter from a church member in her mailbox. The letter writer accused her of being a bad pastor and predicted the sure decline of the church under her leadership. This member had been a thorn in the minister's side for several years, and this correspondence was not the first critical letter the minister had received from this member. Until now, the pastor had always had an immediate response of anger or depression. But this time, the pastor stopped to take a deep breath and to remind herself that she could choose if, when, and how to respond to this assault on her mental and spiritual well-being. She offered the whole relationship up to God in a prayer, including the request to help her forgive the letter writer. Then she was able to put the letter back in its envelope and forget about it until sometime the following week. When she met the letter writer later that morning in the hall, she was able to greet her calmly and wish her a happy Easter. Unfortunately, the member never did come to approve of the pastor, but the pastor was able to move into a healthier place emotionally herself so that she did not allow the member's attacks to control her any longer.

The behavior of groups of leaders, such as sessions, can also have a major impact on how churches react to conflict and anxiety. When the leaders respond to situations thoughtfully and calmly, with open discussion, honesty, and fair-mindedness, problems often disappear or never arise. When the session at St. Luke's decided that an urgent goal of the church was to open the empty church buildings to the community during the week, they went about the task openly and honestly. Soon after they'd identified their goal, a school in the community approached the pastor to ask if it could rent space in the buildings. Over the next months, the session wrestled with the issue. The session members carefully and prayerfully considered both the positive and negative sides of having 150 people using their buildings from 8 a.m. until 6 p.m. five days a week. Finally the session agreed to contract with the school for a generous rent in exchange for the school using certain rooms in the church during the week when no church group was using them.

Over the next months, in spite of constant complaints and emotional eruptions from some people who felt their church was threatened by the school's presence, the session held firm in its resolve. The elders calmly explained to the complainers how they arrived at their decision and listened respectfully to the arguments against having the school in the building. When they led public prayer, they prayed for the school and those connected with it. They told humorous and endearing stories about their interactions with the children. When stewardship season came, they pointed out how helpful it was to have the school's rent money for the budget. They stayed connected to those who objected to their decision, yet they were for the most part able to stand up to their anxiety in nonanxious ways. Over time the great majority of the congregation came to appreciate the school, and even most of those who had resisted its presence grew accustomed to having it there.

The elders in this church were able to be nonanxious in an anxious congregation because they were clear about what they stood for and why. They were able to find spiritual strength in prayer. They earnestly sought God's will through group discernment and had the courage to resist any attempts to sabotage it. They were able to deal calmly and patiently with those who felt threatened, and treated people lovingly through it all. In the end no one left the church or resigned from the session. Throughout this crisis in the church's life, these elders showed themselves to be effective and healthy spiritual leaders.

Much of the work of spiritual leaders is about making decisions that affect the congregation's life. How we go about this work is very important. The next chapter, on the subject of discernment, is about how to have a godly process of decision making as we seek to find and do God's will in the context of church life.

QUESTIONS FOR THOUGHT AND DISCUSSION

1. Some people believe that there should be no conflict in religious organizations. Why do you think this is? Is conflict at church more disturbing than conflict at home or at work?
2. What are the most common causes of anxiety in your congregation?
3. How does change in the congregation stir up anxiety in people? Can you think of an example?
4. Reread the story about Mary, Richard, and John. What would you do if you were John, and why?

9

Discerning Leaders in a Discerning Community

God created human beings with the ability to consider options and make choices. Choices are important because our lives, both personal and corporate, are shaped by our choices and those of others. Christian discernment has to do with making choices that are in accord with God's will. Discernment is important because being Christian is not simply about subscribing to a set of doctrines or religious beliefs. The essence of Christianity is the call to be a disciple and follower of Jesus Christ. It is a call to a Christlike way of life, and this way of life involves choosing to do some things and not to do others.

A true encounter with God always has an impact on a person's actions. Luke's Gospel tells us that when John the Baptist came into the wilderness preaching repentance and baptism, the people who responded to his message asked, "Teacher, what should we do?" (Luke 3:10, 12, 14). After Pentecost, when Peter preached the news of Jesus' resurrection, the people responded by asking, "What should we do?" (Acts 2:37). Jesus clearly expected a certain way of life from his disciples. Those who were baptized had a new identity and were expected to live in this world as citizens of the reign of God. However, Jesus did not leave behind a detailed rule book describing exactly what that new life would look like in every situation.

One of God's gifts to believers is Christian freedom. This freedom is freedom both from something and for something. In baptism we are set free from any necessity to win God's love by following moral or religious rules. God's love is ours already, and we are called to live lives of gratitude and holiness in response. Our freedom is so important to God that God does not compel us to be obedient but rather invites us to follow Jesus each day by making godly choices. In receiving Jesus as Savior and Lord, we are set free from the domination of sin and empowered to choose a different kind of life through the work of the Holy Spirit.

Not every choice in life requires an intentional process of discernment. Many choices for individuals as well as groups are guided by fixed commitments, routine, or common sense. We don't generally pause and discern whether to stop the car at a stop sign or what to have for lunch or whether to pick up the kids from school. Similarly, sometimes the choices required of disciples are very clear. In session meetings, for example, discernment is not necessary to decide whether to approve the minutes or authorize Communion to the homebound. Most of the work of church governing bodies can usually be done by consensus or through a process of prayerful discussion and vote during the meeting. There are, however, significant situations when God's will is not clear to everyone and we must work to understand it. An intentional process of discernment is most appropriate when the matter at hand has long-term consequences, when there are different views on the subject or a variety of choices to be considered, and when the circumstances allow time for working through the matter instead of requiring a quick decision.

This work of discernment has been part of the Christian life from the beginning. In the early days of the faith, for instance, as non-Jews began to be converted, there were different opinions in the church about how they should be received. Did they have to become Jews before they became Christians, or could they simply confess Jesus and be baptized? In the book of Acts, we see the church working to discern God's will on this matter. In the midst of conflicting ideas about what should be done, the church turned to the Scriptures, to prayer, and to a process of listening to each other's insights and experiences (see Acts 10, 11, and 15 for the whole story). The clear implication of the text is that the Holy Spirit sent by Jesus guided the church through this experience and led these believers to a decision in line with God's will.

Since that time, Christians have worked to discern the path of faithfulness, believing that

—God is the creator, redeemer, and sustainer of this world and therefore its rightful ruler.

—God's will for us is good will, and we can trust God's faithfulness in good times and in bad.

—God cares what we do and calls us to live in this world in ways that advance God's will being done on earth as it is in heaven.

—The God who calls us into discipleship will give us the resources, guidance, and spiritual power to do God's will.

—The power and grace of God are made manifest in our weakness, so that God can redeem our mistakes and use our failures for God's glory and purposes.

—The prime goal of discernment is not attaining moral perfection but rather partnering with God in the ongoing reconciliation of the world.

WHAT DOES "GOD'S WILL" MEAN?

The subject of discernment can make us uncomfortable because it includes the idea of God's will. Some wonder whether we can actually know God's particular will in any given situation. What about all the evil that has been done through the centuries by people who thought they were doing God's will? How can we be sure we are doing God's will and not our own? Theological tomes have been written on these questions, and I do not intend to write another one here. However, if we desire a discerning way of life, having a basic working understanding of what we mean by the phrase "God's will" is important.

At the heart of the concept of God's will is the truth that God cares about what we do. Our choices matter to God because we, as individuals and communities, matter to God. God loves us, and that love has been expressed in its highest form in Jesus Christ, who showed us God's love and God's will in everything he did and said. Christians are called to let our actions be shaped on a daily basis both by the witness to Christ that we have in Scripture and by the living presence of his Holy Spirit.

Finding God's will is not a game of hide-and-seek with God hiding and us seeking. The truth is that we already know more of God's will than we are often willing to undertake. We know that it is God's will that we love our enemies, turn the other cheek when attacked, forgive and pray for those who injure us, and reject opportunities for revenge. We know it is God's will that we live a moderate, healthful, modest life, being good stewards of our health and treating our bodies as temples of the Holy Spirit. We know that we are called to give sacrificially, beginning with a tithe of our income, so that God's work may go forward. We know we are to serve Christ by serving people who are poor, sick, imprisoned, naked, hungry, and friendless. We know that we are called to be peacemakers in a world full of conflict and violence. We know that we are commissioned as witnesses of the gospel to those around us and even to the ends of the earth. We know we are to live in all things a life worthy of our calling as salt and light in the world. These precepts and many others like them are stated in the Bible.

Discipleship involves attuning ourselves day by day to God's will as we know it in Scripture and claiming the Spirit's resources to empower us to do it. More than anything else the daily struggle to make Christ-like choices and to order our lives and communities in line with God's will shapes us into discerning people. Those who practice this discipline come into the process of communal decision making, such as a session meeting, equipped to listen for God's will for the church. They know the voice of God in the "sound of sheer silence" (1 Kgs. 19:12). They trust the Spirit to lead them and are committed to follow. They do not allow worries and anxieties to rush them into premature decision making. Gathered as the people of God, they test all discernments by God's perfect word: Jesus Christ as revealed in Scripture interpreted by the Holy Spirit.

When faced with discernment around a particular issue, many well-intentioned Christians are paralyzed by the fear of making a mistake. Underlying this fear may be the idea that God's will is like a bull's-eye on a target and that in order to please God we have to hit it perfectly. Maybe it is better to refuse to engage in discernment than to risk arriving at the wrong answer. Psalm 103 provides a healthy corrective: "As a father has compassion for his children, so the LORD has compassion for those who fear him. For he knows how we were made; he remembers that we are dust" (Ps. 103:13–14). God does not expect perfection. God expects us to do our best to live as faithful disciples. God knows that our choices and actions will often be flawed because we are flawed creatures, but God is delighted by our attempts to know and do God's will, and like a loving parent, God has mercy on our failures.

In thinking about God's will, it is also helpful to remember that God is already at work in the world in ways too numerous to count. Instead of hitting the bull's-eye, perhaps seeking God's will means listening to the sounds and signs of God at work in the world and being willing to get in the flow of what God is already doing. Instead of picturing God's will as a bull's-eye we must hit, why not think of it as finding where the rivers of God's will are already flowing in the world and allowing ourselves to be carried forward by the flow of the current?

This is an image of commitment and faith. To enter the flow of a river means that we will not stay in the same place. As the river flows along, sometimes the ride will be placid; sometimes it will be rough. Our task is not to direct the river or make it flow, but rather to take our place in the current. While far from a perfect metaphor for seeking God's will, this image captures the truth that discernment of God's call is an ongoing way of life. It reminds us that we are engaged in a process that God is directing. This way of understanding God's will requires more from us than an exercise in hitting the bull's-eye from time to time when important matters arise. When spiritual leaders make the commitment to stay in the flow of God's will no matter where it leads, church becomes an adventure.

THE MARKS OF DISCERNMENT

A discerning way of life has certain characteristics. You may be familiar with some of them already and practicing them yourself or in a group:

1. *Discernment is God-focused.* The focus of discernment is always on God. The key questions are: What is God's call to us? What is God's desire in this situation? The important assumption here is that God will make God's desire known to us as we pray, listen, and search. The God Jesus showed us is a God eager to be self-revealing. Jesus urged his disciples to ask, seek, and knock, assuring them that by God's grace what they needed would be given to them.

Discernment also brings us face to face with the call to surrender ourselves fully to God. We can only partner with God in God's work to the degree we are willing to let God take the lead and do what only God can do. Too often we assume we know what God wants, and we set out to do it with perhaps a little prayer for God to help us. This approach may stir up a whirlwind of activity, engage numbers of people in programs, and even do some good in the world. However, these efforts usually bear little lasting fruit. Practicing discernment reminds us that every day we are first and foremost to be about the task of seeking God's will, not our own. This may keep us from falling into the temptation to make God a means to our own ends.

2. *Discernment requires faith.* The desire to know and to do God's will is in itself a gift of the Holy Spirit. If we have this desire, we claim by faith that God is already at work in us to lead our decision making. Discernment is not something we produce, but rather something God does in us. When we recognize it happening in or among us, we praise God, who is the source of every good gift. One of the beautiful things about a discerning way of life is that it keeps us constantly turned toward God. It relieves us of the tyranny of circumstances, the obsession with personalities and politics, and the addiction to always having our way. Instead we all turn as one to face the One who promises to lead us if we are willing to be led.

The writer of Proverbs calls on the people to "trust in the LORD with all your heart, and do not rely on your own insight. In all your ways acknowledge him, and he will make straight your paths" (Prov. 3:5–6). In faith we are called to trust God beyond that which we can see. Sometimes when we engage in a process of discernment, the answer that comes seems beyond possibility. Are we willing to follow where God seems to be pointing us even when we cannot see the way ahead?

Some years ago I was pastor of a congregation that discerned the need to call additional staff to broaden its ministry into the community. We had a certain amount of money to fund the ministry on a part-time basis for a number of years. However, as the search for the new staff person unfolded, the person who seemed most clearly gifted and called to the position could not afford to work part-time and would have to move to us from a faraway state. In a process that took more than a year, the search committee and the candidate for the position worked to discern God's will. In the end both the church and the minister (along with spouse and children!) took a leap of faith and moved forward into this adventure in spite of the obstacles. Each year money appeared to fund this work either through unexpected gifts or increased giving by members and new members. The willingness to take this leap of faith resulted in a ministry that bore good fruit for the congregation, the community, and the family that answered this call. Those who take up the task of discernment should be aware that they may be led outside of their comfort zone and involved in actions that at the time may make little sense on a strictly logical level.

3. *Discernment is communal.* When we make medical decisions, we want our doctor to give us the most up-to-date advice based on medical research and accepted protocols. When we have a legal problem, we expect our attorney to be well versed in all the law of the land. When

we have an ethical issue, we go to our pastor or trusted wise counselor to hear his or her thoughts on the matter. Similarly, the process of making decisions through Christian discernment draws us out of ourselves and requires us to seek the best wisdom we can from our tradition and our community.

Presbyterians turn first to the Bible, for as the Westminster Larger Catechism teaches, "The holy Scriptures of the Old and New Testaments are the Word of God, the only rule of faith and obedience."[1] While most Christians would agree that the Bible is meant to guide how we believe and therefore live, understanding what Scripture requires of us in particular circumstances requires reflection and interpretation. For instance, how does Scripture come into play when a session is discerning whether or not to sell its current property and move to another place? Instead of flipping through the Bible looking for yes or no answers, Presbyterians believe that we can discern God's will on this matter by taking time to reflect prayerfully on the circumstances, the whole message of Scripture, and how it applies to our situation. As the Holy Spirit moves in this process, in the fullness of time a path of faithfulness will be made clear enough, and we wait until it is.

To help us in this interpretation process, we can look to the historic theological documents in the *Book of Confessions*. They contain the testimony of Christians in generations past who struggled to interpret Scripture and discern God's will in many circumstances and on many subjects. We are not the first Christians to seek God's will. Listening to the testimony of the great cloud of witnesses represented in the confessions can shed significant spiritual light on our path.

Spiritual guidance also comes to us through each other. As groups discuss and pray, insight will often come through the Holy Spirit working through the minds and spirits of the group members. Discernment requires that we honor the contributions of others and listen for God's truth to come from them, even though we may disagree with some of what they say. Special people in every community of faith have unusually deep insights into the things of God. Steeped in prayer, grounded in Scripture, and gifted with wisdom from the Holy Spirit, these people are great resources in times of discernment. Having the humility to seek guidance from others is essential to good discernment. Likewise we can be guided through the wisdom of people we have never met personally through books, articles, printed or recorded lectures, or sermons. Sometimes an image, a story, a verse of Scripture, or even a single word opens the way forward.

THE HOLY SPIRIT AND DISCERNMENT

At the center of the practice of discernment is the expectation that God's Spirit will lead us as we seek God's will. Jesus stressed God's readiness to help believers by promising, "If you then, who are evil [sinful], know how to give good gifts to your children, how much more will the heavenly Father give the Holy Spirit to those who ask" (Luke 11:13). True Christian discernment can happen only as we claim Jesus' promise and open ourselves to the Holy Spirit's work in our midst. This openness often requires the humility to let go of our desires so that we might be open to God's desire, whatever that may turn out to be. We must be very careful not to fall into thinking of the Holy Spirit as a means to our ends, no matter how good those ends might be. The Spirit is not a religious tool that we use to get something done for God. Instead, the Holy Spirit uses us to the end that God's will is done on earth as it is in heaven. How does the Holy Spirit work in the community of believers who seek God's will?

First, *the Holy Spirit is the power source of the believing community.* The first disciples were not a particularly impressive group in their own right. They were not the movers and shakers of Jerusalem. They were mostly ordinary folk who fished for a living or collected taxes or kept house. They were drawn together by their attraction to Jesus, but at times their understanding of what Jesus was about seemed dim and their faith weak. Even after the resurrection, as Jesus was about to ascend into heaven, the disciples were still fixed on their own agendas. "They asked him, 'Lord, is this the time when you will restore the kingdom to Israel?' He replied, 'It is not for you to know the times or periods that the Father has set by his own authority. *But you will receive power* when the Holy Spirit has come upon you; and you will be my witnesses in Jerusalem, in all Judea and Samaria, and to the ends of the earth'" (Acts 1:6–8; emphasis added). Jesus shifted the focus from their own political goals to the task of being witnesses for him and promised them the power they will need to carry out this work.

In obedience to Jesus' direction, the believers went back to Jerusalem and waited, praying and fasting until the day of Pentecost. On that day the power of God was poured out on the believing community, and the wind of the Spirit blew them out of the upper room to transform the world. The story of the early church in Acts is the story of the Holy Spirit empowering these ordinary people to do the things Jesus did and even greater things than he did (John 13:12).

Those who seek to do God's will today are still dependent on the power of God's Holy Spirit. God's power can draw us together when, left to our own devices, we would remain divided. God can show us the way forward when it seems that every way is blocked. God can open doors that on a human level are firmly closed. God can change people's minds and soften hard hearts. God can draw people with needed gifts into our churches in order to enable us to carry forward a particular mission. God can give us strength beyond human strength, and when our bank accounts are insufficient, God is able to send the resources we need to do what we are called to do. Our faith that the Spirit who empowered and resourced the first disciples is eager to do the same for us today frees us to discern and obey God's will with joyous abandon.

The Spirit is also our teacher. Jesus says that "the Advocate, the Holy Spirit, whom the Father will send in my name, will teach you everything, and remind you of all that I have said to you" (John 14:26). The Spirit brings to our memory what Jesus taught and did and helps us make connections between his witness and our situation. So often when we are faced with difficult decisions, our minds become fixed on the problem to the extent that we become distracted and discouraged. The Spirit works to bring to our memory treasures of the faith that can restore our focus and help us see God's will more clearly.

The Holy Spirit is *"the Spirit of truth*, whom the world cannot receive, because it neither sees him nor knows him" (John 14:17; emphasis added). Truth here does not refer to truth in a general sense, but rather to God's truth. Another way to understand this is to say that the Holy Spirit gives us glimpses of the world as God sees it and as God wants it to be. The Spirit enables us to see beyond the blinders of custom and culture and self-interest to catch a vision of things from God's perspective. Here again, Scripture is our main source for understanding God's truth. The Spirit works in our minds and hearts as we read and interpret Scripture together. We begin to understand how God's eternal truth can take shape in our time and our situation and to see what faithfulness requires of us.

For example, Jesus commissioned his disciples to go out into the world and make disciples of all nations. The book of Acts tells us the story of how the first disciples lived out this commission in their first-century world. But what does it look like when twenty-first-century believers attempt to be faithful to that commission, and especially, what is God calling our particular church to do to make disciples in our community and to the ends of the earth? Using sanctified imagination and listening for the Spirit's guidance, each faith community is called to see its context through God's eyes and catch a vision of what God wants it to be doing.

The Holy Spirit is our Advocate. Jesus said to his disciples on the night he was betrayed, "I will not leave you orphaned" (John 14:18); "I will ask the Father, and he will give you another Advocate, to be with you forever" (John 14:16). The Greek word translated into English here as advocate or helper carries the image of someone standing with another person in a court of law or some other threatening situation. The idea is that the circumstances require more than we can provide for ourselves. We need someone with influence and authority to accompany us and to work on our behalf.

Whenever believers in Christ are called into challenging situations, the Holy Spirit stands beside us to support us. We are never alone. We are never without resources. We do not have to let anxiety and worry dominate our lives. For example, Jesus made this promise to disciples called to give account of their faith in time of trial: "Do not worry beforehand about what you are to say; but say whatever is given you at that time, for it is not you who speak, but the Holy Spirit" (Mark 13:11). The Advocate will supply the very words we need to make a faithful witness.

The Spirit also helps us pray. There are times when we cannot find the words to pray what is in us. Sometimes we are too weak, sick, or depressed to pray. At other times we may not even be able to know what is the best thing for which to pray. In these situations when we have no ability to form a prayer, the "Spirit intercedes with sighs too deep for words. And God, who searches the heart, knows what is the mind of the Spirit, because the Spirit intercedes for the saints according to the will of God" (Rom. 8:26–27). In the process of discernment, it is empowering and comforting to know that the Holy Spirit is standing with us, praying our need and claiming God's supply.

Prayer is at the heart of discernment and more than anything else serves to make it a transforming practice for individuals and communities. But it is important to understand how prayer functions in discernment. There is not a set of correct prayer words that unlock the secrets of God. Neither is prayer like making deposits in a spiritual bank account so that when we reach a certain level God does what we want. There is no guarantee that if we pray enough or in the "right" way, things will go our way. Instead, prayer is about relationship. It is a means of connecting with the living God we know in Jesus, and this kind of relationship is always transforming. In prayer we put ourselves where God can get at us; we surrender ourselves to the One who loved us and died for us.

In the context of discernment, prayer is not telling God what to do but rather opening ourselves to receive what God wants to do in, for, and through us. Prayer can be thought of as opening doors through which the grace of God can flow to us, to other people, into the church and the world. We don't control where the grace goes; we don't always get what we want. However, at the same time we participate in what God wants to do in the world, and we ourselves are transformed by the power of the Holy Spirit. So it is that the fruit of Christian discernment is not just godly decisions, but also godly people.

The Holy Spirit gives peace. Believers also find such peace is beyond anything the world can give. We see this peace being lived out in the Garden of Gethsemane as Jesus looked the horror of the cross in the face and prayed to be released from it, struggling so fiercely that sweat fell from his face like great drops of blood (Luke 22:44). Yet in the midst of his struggle, we hear him letting go of his will to grasp God's will. He received the peace that passes all understanding, and this Spirit-given peace sustained him through his arrest, trial, and crucifixion, even unto death.

The peace that the world gives is a fragile thing built on a foundation of favorable circumstances, plentiful resources, success, and good fortune. The peace that the Holy Spirit brings to believers, on the other hand, flourishes in the hardscrabble soil of failure, danger, weakness, and lack. This peace is built on a firm foundation of trust and hope in God, who never forsakes the believer. As the Holy Spirit gives us this peace, we are empowered to take risks and leaps of faith for God's sake that those who only see with worldly eyes will never understand. Peace comes not because we are strong, but because the Holy Spirit enables us to believe that God is strong. As Martin Luther's great hymn says, "We will not fear, for God has willed God's truth to triumph through us."[2]

Discernment is not primarily a technique we learn, but rather a way of life. It is a practice that serves to develop in us a Christian character. As with all spiritual practices, the goal of discernment is that little by little we come to embody the gospel and become obedient partners in God's work in the world. The New Testament speaks of this process in terms of having our minds set on the Spirit (Rom. 8:5), living by the Spirit and being led by the Spirit (Gal. 5:16, 18), and bearing the image of the man of heaven (Christ) (1 Cor. 15:49). Other Scriptures speak in communal terms of the whole Christian community being transformed. In Romans 12:1–2, the writer uses Greek plural pronouns (you all) to encourage the entire church not to be conformed to this world, but instead to be transformed by the renewing of their minds through the daily practice of offering their bodies as living sacrifices. Spiritual leaders are especially called to be involved in this process of transformation, claiming by faith the promise that God who never forsakes the faithful will guide, resource, and redeem their efforts.

QUESTIONS FOR THOUGHT AND DISCUSSION

1. How would you define "God's will" to a thirteen-year-old member of the confirmation class?
2. What is one area of your life where the choices you make and have made are largely determined by what you believe to be God's will? How have your beliefs about God's will shaped your choices?
3. How do you experience the power of the Holy Spirit at work in your life as you seek to know and do God's will?
4. This chapter mentions images of hitting a bull's-eye and being carried by a river as ways to understanding what it means to do God's will. Which of these images is more helpful to you and why?
5. According to the book of Acts, the early church was guided and empowered by God, specifically through the actions of the Holy Spirit. Is it possible for churches today to have this kind of experience? What areas of your church's life could benefit from some empowering by the Holy Spirit?

10

The Care and Feeding of Spiritual Leaders

Sue Allen, a member of the officer nominating committee at Calvary Church, has volunteered to call two potential officer candidates to ask if they would meet to discuss possibly serving on the session next year. Her first call is to Tim Hayes, who has served on session before in a different congregation. Tim is delighted about the possibility of being an active elder at Calvary and tells Sue, "Serving as an elder helped me grow in my faith more than anything else I have ever done in the church." They set a time to meet, and Sue promises to give Tim some written information Sunday about what being on the session of Calvary Church entails.

Next Sue calls Dawn Anderson. Dawn served as an active elder at Calvary about ten years ago, and although she had turned down several invitations to consider serving again, the nominating committee is eager to have her back on the session. When Sue makes her request on behalf of the committee, Dawn is silent for a long moment. Then she shares with Sue that her last experience on session left her feeling frustrated, discouraged, and spiritually depleted. Dawn concludes by telling Sue, "When my term was over, I swore I would never serve on session again." Sue was left pondering these two very different experiences and wondering what could be done to help officers end their terms of service feeling more like Tim and less like Dawn.

There is no simple formula for ensuring that all church officers become effective leaders, grow in discipleship to Christ, and have stronger relationships with their congregation and with God at the end of their terms than they had when they started. There are, however, practices that tend in that direction. The scope of this chapter does not allow for a full exploration of all these practices. Instead I lift up some of the most important ones and give some ideas to start you thinking about how to help officers succeed and grow.

The work of developing and supporting spiritual leaders in a church is a shared responsibility; pastors, sessions (and boards of deacons, if applicable), and members of the congregation all have their parts to play. Some things only the officer herself or himself can do. As these nurturing practices and the attitudes that support them work their way into the fabric of a congregation's life, a climate will be created in which spiritual leaders are more likely to flourish.

WHAT CHURCHES CAN DO TO SUPPORT AND NURTURE OFFICERS

All churches desire high functioning officers who are effective spiritual leaders. Following are a number of things churches can do to move toward this goal.

Work on the Nominating Committee Process

In some ways the officer nominating committee is the most important committee in the church. It may even have as much long-term impact on the life of the congregation as the session does, because it nominates those who will be on the session (and the board of deacons, if a church has one). The stage for many an officer's good or not-so-good experience is set as the nominating committee does its job.

Of first importance is the question of how the committee understands the work it is elected to do. Its task is not simply to find people willing to fill slots on the ballot for elders or deacons! It is better to leave one or more positions unfilled for a while than to nominate to the congregation someone who is unqualified or unenthusiastic about serving. Rather, good nominating committees work on discerning the congregation's leadership needs and the members who have the wherewithal to meet those needs. The elder serving as moderator of the nominating committee should make sure that a portion of the first meeting is given over to explaining the importance and focus of the committee's work. At this point the pastor (as ex officio member of the nominating committee) can also give helpful theological and biblical grounding about discerning the call to leadership and recognizing spiritual gifts and talents that the church needs.

Wrapping prayer into every stage of the nominating committee's work enables the committee to keep its focus on doing God's work and also opens doors for God's grace to flow into the whole process. Members of the committee can be urged to pray through the membership directory as part of their preparation. Beyond the custom of opening and closing meetings with prayer, it is also helpful to take time out during the meetings at various points to pray for God's guidance. Visits and phone calls to prospective officers should be surrounded with prayer. Think about recruiting a small prayer team of church members to support the work of the nominating committee, keeping names and details confidential but sharing general information about the process to guide the prayers. The congregation should be encouraged each week in worship and whenever churchwide concerns are shared to remember the work of the nominating committee in its prayers.

How a nominating committee communicates with its prospects is very important, and the quality of the contact does much either to honor or to devalue the office of elder or deacon in the congregation. Grabbing someone in the hallway at church on Sunday and asking them to serve as an officer says, "This office and your decision about serving are not very significant." Making an appointment for two members of the nominating committee to talk with the nominee, especially outside the church, says, "This work is important, and your decision about it is very important to us, to the church, and to God." Scheduling personal visits with potential nominees also signals that a serious commitment is being asked of them. People need to know that spiritual leadership must be a priority, not just one more activity that finds its place somewhere down the list of life's obligations. If possible, the nominating committee should be able to say to a prospective nominee, "This is how we see your spiritual gifts and your talents fitting into our church's mission plan, and here is how we envision your involvement." This approach clearly says, "We have considered this matter deeply, and we believe that you have a call from God to do this particular work."

When the nominating committee members meet with a prospective officer, they should be as honest and explicit as possible about what being an elder or deacon requires in terms of time, meetings to attend, and work to be done. Unpleasant surprises after nominees have made a commitment before God and the church can sap an officer's energy and joy. A written explanation about the office of elder or deacon and what participation on the session or board of deacons requires should be given to the potential nominee in advance of the personal visit. In setting up the appointment the nominating committee members should allow the nominee time to reflect and pray over the matter. A written explanation also gives the nominee something to go back to after the meeting as she or he works through her or his decision.

Provide Training and Spiritual Growth Resources to All Officers

The amount of time invested in training and providing continuing education for officers is a good indication of the degree to which pastors and sessions value the ministry and leadership of lay leaders. To put someone into the role of church officer without adequate training and support is to invite them to commit malpractice in spiritual leadership. After all, the oversight of the whole congregation is being placed into their hands, so that along with the pastor, the officers are responsible for the health and growth of the congregation. Officers being newly ordained need a minimum of ten to twelve hours of training. Veteran officers being called to serve again should be asked to attend appropriate parts of the training and to help teach the training by sharing with the new officers what they have learned previously. When persuading veteran elders to attend training, it is helpful to remind them that the *Book of Order* has changed since they last served (it changes every two years). Attending parts of the training also lets veteran officers build relationships with the other active elders.

A basic officer training course should include, first, an exploration of an officer-elect's faith journey. They should be helped to develop the ability to state their beliefs and give witness to how God has made a difference in their lives. An introduction to church history gives officers a sense of our spiritual roots and a reminder that we are not the first Christians (or Presbyterians!) who ever lived. Training in basic Reformed theology and polity is necessary so that officers can answer the ordination questions truthfully and go about their work guided by Scripture as interpreted by our confessions and polity. This part of the training should include instruction in a Reformed understanding of Scripture and how to interpret it. Before training classes dealing with polity and confessions, assigned readings in the *Book of Confessions* and *Book of Order* help prepare new officers to understand the material. A unit on the mission of the church and how we all work together within the Presbyterian Church (U.S.A.) to do God's work is essential.

These classes can be taught outside the local congregation in groups sponsored by presbyteries or regional cluster groups. This practice is good stewardship of time and energy and also builds relationships with other congregations. There are a variety of resources available through our denomination's Presbyterian Publishing Corporation and through the Office of Theology and Worship in Louisville as resources for those teaching officer training. Some presbyteries in areas where congregations are few and far between are experimenting with long-distance education through videoconferencing or are producing computer resources or DVDs that can be used for officer training in local churches.

Along with the subjects mentioned above, it is important for officers, pastor(s), and staff to meet at the local church level to delve into what it means to be an officer in that particular congregation. Information shared should include what is expected of officers, how to participate effectively in session meetings, how all the committees of the church work together, any important issues going on in the congregation, and other practical knowledge. New officers also need to know such simple things as how to get into the church buildings after hours; how to be reimbursed for expenses; what they can expect the church staff to do for them and what they need to do for themselves; dates, times, and locations of session or deacon board meetings; where their church mailbox is; and how to communicate information to the church at large. We set new people up to be ineffective if we assume they already know these things.

Officer training is also the place where pastors can begin to build strong personal and working relationship with officers. These relationships lay the foundation for trust, good communication, and effective teamwork in the future. When trouble or conflict arises, officers and pastors will find that time spent in building trust and mutual understanding was time well spent. Investing in training and building relationships with elders and deacons is one of the best investments a pastor can make in the health of a congregation.

Even after substantial initial training, spiritual leaders need continuing education and opportunities for team building and spiritual growth. The *Book of Order* lays upon the session the responsibility for making sure this equipping happens; the session may choose to delegate the planning to the pastor or other staff members. Annual or bian-nual session/board of deacons retreats is one way to give officers ongo-ing education and inspiration. Additionally, officers might agree to read books, articles, or perhaps portions of the *Book of Confessions* together and set aside time to discuss them in session or deacons' meetings. Activities such as special seasons of corporate and personal prayer can help officers access the spiritual resources for their work and have major impact on the life of the congregation. A Communion service as part of the session meeting several times a year can be a means of grace for church leaders. The possibilities for creativity are many. No matter how it happens, the purpose of this continuing nurture is to keep filling the spiritual and theological well so that elders and deacons may draw the resources they need to grow in faith and to fulfill their ministries.

Create a Positive Climate for Lay Spiritual Leadership

The attitude of the pastor(s) has a major impact on the climate sur-rounding lay leadership in the congregation. If a pastor acts and speaks as if she or he is *the* spiritual leader in the church, the officers generally begin to abdicate that role. Over time officers forget the true nature of their calling. They settle for being program directors who carry out the pastor's vision and plans. However, if a pastor regularly reminds elders and deacons that they are spiritual leaders, teaches them how to func-tion as spiritual leaders and resources them in this ministry, uses them in pastoral care and worship, and involves them in visioning and mis-sion planning, little by little a space will be created for strong ministry by the church's lay officers.

The concept of the pastor and officers serving together as a spiritual leadership team for the church is a powerful concept to use in creating a good climate for lay leadership. Pastors can model speaking of the ses-sion and board of deacons in this way in sermons, announcements, and conversations with church members. Using more "we" language and less "I" language in meetings is also a way to say to officers, "We are all in this together." Making decisions through the process of communal discernment when appropriate, rather than simply by discussion and voting, gives officers a chance to practice working together as a team.

Another practice that helps create a positive climate for lay leader-ship is sharing information as widely as possible among the officers. Being the last to find out important information makes people feel unimportant and devalued. Effective information sharing does not just happen; it must be intentionally woven into the life of the church. The selective use of e-mail or automatic phone message systems to keep officers aware of developments can be very helpful. If committees produce written minutes or reports, sharing them (or a summary version) with the whole session is a good practice unless there is some particular reason not to. Blindsiding people with unpleasant information, especially in a meeting, should be avoided at all costs.

Pastors who want to empower others as spiritual leaders may find it helpful to practice a less directive and more collegial leadership style when circumstances allow. Offering a number of options instead of only one and discussing the possible consequences of various options helps leaders practice decision-making skills. Allowing time and space in meetings for creativity and solutions to problems to bubble up from the group rather than always driving toward a quick decision can tend to empower leaders.

Another factor in the development of laypersons as spiritual leaders is the degree to which they receive personal support and spiritual care and counsel along the way, especially when they face difficulties. One of the causes of burnout among church officers is a combination of trouble at work or trouble at home combined with a challenging situation at church. Pastors and other pastoral caregivers can help by keeping in close personal touch with the church's officers and making sure they receive encouragement and care when needed. Pastors may find that trying times are excellent opportunities to deepen relationships with officers and to offer spiritual guidance that deepens faith. When elders and deacons find that they can count on encouragement, prayer, and substantive assistance from their church in struggle and difficulty, they are encouraged to serve through hard times and find that their faith and Christian character are strengthened.

Coordinate and Organize Tasks to Help Officers Succeed

In many congregations, individual church officers are responsible for overseeing major portions of the congregation's ministry. Fellowship, education, mission, worship, evangelism, finances and stewardship, and property matters are often under the care of groups led by church officers. To help these officers succeed in this part of their responsibility, fitting the right person to each task is important. This matching is not as easy as it might sound. I once heard from an irate elder-elect, a teacher by profession, who felt she was not being taken seriously because she had been assigned to the education committee. Her real passion was mission, and she wanted to serve in that area. On the other hand, assigning an accountant to the worship committee may leave him feeling like a fish out of water with no way to use his best talents and gifts.

Giving people choices is generally the best practice. Instead of simply assigning people to areas of responsibility, try asking new officers to name three or four areas where they would like to serve. Beware of trying to fit someone with no aptitude or interest into a particular job just because no one else is available to do it. It is better to let some things fall by the wayside or to rearrange the responsibilities of others to find the right fit for the work that needs to be done.

One of the causes of burnout among lay leaders is that the task to which they are assigned is either too big or not challenging enough. If the task is too large, the leader may feel overwhelmed and want to give up. This is a danger especially for those who do not know how to delegate or are reluctant to ask others to help. When the work does not get done or it is done poorly, the officer in charge may be discouraged and embarrassed. Sometimes they leave the church feeling shamed or unappreciated. Other officers may become bored when they are given assignments that they consider to be insignificant. They want a challenge and will feel that their time is being wasted unless they get one. Again, using discernment to match an officer's gifts and passions with the church's mission is the best practice.

Regular opportunities for officers and their committees to evaluate their work and learn from experience are growth producing. One church I served held an evaluation meeting the week after the annual vacation Bible school was over to talk about the experience and make notes for next year. This practice helped weed out things about the program that did not work and was also a chance for new ideas to emerge. The notes of this meeting were given to the director for the coming year's Bible school. Such opportunities for regular evaluation help leaders become accustomed to self-critique and learn how to profit from it. If evaluation never happens, organizations tend to do the same things over and over again, even if they are far from excellent.

Officers need to know what they and their committees have authority to do and what activities or actions the session must authorize. A best practice here is to come up with a commonly agreed-upon list of things the committees need to bring to the session for a vote and which things can simply be reported as information. It is also very helpful for each officer to know exactly how much money in the church budget is allotted to her or his area of responsibility. Few things are more frustrating than not knowing how much money is available to use for work that needs to be done. Regular financial reports, preferably monthly, help officers stay on top of what they have spent and how much they still have available for the work ahead. Providing clear information about lines of authority and finances is an important part of organizing the work of the session and deacons so that leaders can succeed.

Celebrate and Show Appreciation

People are encouraged in their service to God through the mission of the church when they know their work is significant and they feel appreciated. People who bear the burdens of leadership especially need encouragement and appreciation. Those who want to build up the ministry of church officers will find frequent opportunities to bring their accomplishments to the attention of the congregation and celebrate them. While the glory always goes to God, celebrating the good things that have been achieved encourages the faithful and is a witness to uninvolved people of the joy found in doing God's work.

Likewise, one of the most powerful encouragements a church can provide to its spiritual leaders is to be intentional and regular about thanking them for their service. One congregation assigned each elder an "angel" from the congregation. This person committed to pray for the elder, to remember his or her birthday, and to make encouraging contacts on a regular basis. Other congregations hold Officer Appreciation Days every couple of years so that, during a three-year term, all officers will experience such an occasion. Teachers can talk to the Sunday school classes about the work of the elders and deacons and have the children make thank-you cards to give to each officer. Even remembering to say to an officer, "I appreciate what you do," in the hallway at church is encouraging.

Pastors also need to express genuine appreciation for the service of the officers (and vice versa!). A good investment of time is for the pastor or a member of the pastoral staff to have a personal visit at least annually with each elder or deacon. These visits should have no other agenda than asking, "How are you doing?" and expressing appreciation for her or his service. Officers' birthdays are great occasions for such visits.

Officers likewise can encourage pastors by making sure they know they are valued for their work and for themselves. Feeling appreciated often makes us want to do more; feeling unappreciated can lead to discouragement and bitterness.

WAYS OFFICERS CAN PRACTICE
SOUL-CARE AND SELF-CARE

1. *Remember why you do what you do.* As we explored in chapter 7, the church is both a human and a divine institution. Along with the sacred business of the body of Christ, as leaders we are also involved in many human concerns that can be exhausting and frustrating. In fact, the two are so often mixed together that it is hard to tell the difference. Disagreement is a fact of life in the church, and leaders have a role to play in settling or managing it. There are difficult personalities to deal with and difficult problems to solve. Sometimes good intentions backfire, leaving hurt feelings and grudges. Often we are frustrated because the resources we have don't begin to cover what we want to do. Sometimes they don't even cover the necessities.

Why *do* we do what we do in the church? Is it to make the world a better place? Is it to make the church better? Is it to meet people's needs? Is it to live a life that pleases God? Is it because we can't say no? Is it because we know every person has to pull one's share of the load? Many of us who give our time and effort in church leadership seldom stop to think about why we do it. Often we are so busy fulfilling our obligations that we don't have time to think. For the sake of our spiritual health, however, it is a good practice to pause from time to time and get back in touch with our deepest motivations for the work of spiritual leadership.

One of the most basic Christian doctrines is that of salvation by grace through faith. It teaches that God always makes the first move in the human-divine relationship. God is always seeking to save and heal and bless us. God goes before us and meets us with love in every life situation. The fact that God loves us makes us valuable and worthy. We do nothing to earn this love; it is a gift freely given by God, not because we deserve it, but because God loves to love, forgive, and bless.

As we walk daily in this relationship with God, our lives are transformed. We become more sensitive to God's presence with us, and we begin to have a desire to serve God out of gratitude. We answer God's

call as a way of giving ourselves back to the One who has given us everything. Among all of the motivations for answering the call to be church
leaders, this one is the most life-giving and empowering. In times of
stress and frustration it is good to lay hold of this truth afresh.

One way to refresh your sense of call is to go back and remember
your history with God. You can take this step in an organized way by
dividing your life into decades or life stages and taking time to reflect
on how God blessed you in your twenties, forties, and sixties, or as a
child, a teenager, young adult, and so on. Take a piece of paper, and for
each stage or age write down major events that happened to you, how
you experienced God's presence in your life during that time, who the
people were whom God used to bless you, and how you can see God's
good providence at work during that period of your life. This simple
exercise can help you regain your perspective and can open up an ener-
gizing well of gratitude in your heart and mind.

Another good way to keep your spiritual focus sharp is to remember
on a regular basis the events surrounding your call. Go back and recall
what it felt like to have the pastor's and elders' hands on your head during ordination. Reflect on the questions you were asked at your ordination and installation. They are found in the Form of Government in
the *Book of Order*. Remember the times when you felt most deeply
related to God and to the church, when you felt used to do God's work.
In trying times, it is good to grasp anew the truth that you are not simply doing volunteer work. Rather you are answering a call to serve the
Lord and head of the church, Jesus Christ. You serve Christ as you serve
the church and do God's work in the world.

Remembering that we are not called to be everything to everybody
can also help us deal with the frustrations of our calling. Our ultimate
responsibility is to Jesus, not to the members of the church. Jesus offers
to provide what we need to do the job he wants done. Wearing his yoke
is the way to freedom; wearing the yoke of the congregation is the way
to burnout.

2. *Recognize your dependence on God.* Shortly before his crucifixion,
Jesus said to his disciples, "Abide in me as I abide in you. Just as the
branch cannot bear fruit by itself unless it abides in the vine, neither
can you unless you abide in me. I am the vine, you are the branches.
Those who abide in me and I in them bear much fruit, because apart
from me you can do nothing" (John 15:4–5). Using an agricultural
image, Jesus instructs his disciples about the crucial connection
between his presence in their lives and their ability to do his work. The

root of the Greek word translated here as "abide" suggests setting up a tent and living beside someone. The focus in this commandment is the life-giving relationship between Jesus Christ and the believer.

Spiritual leaders are called to bear fruit. We look for results that change people's lives, our world, and our church for the better. The question is where does such fruit come from? Does it come from our efforts, or does God do it? Jesus' words about vines and branches point beyond the "who does what" question to a vital organic relationship between believer and God, disciple and Lord. If this relationship is close, the disciples will bear fruit. If it is not close enough to be life-giving, there will be no fruit, or at least not fruit that will last (John 15:16).

How do we get this kind of relationship with God? Jesus tells us that it is ours for the asking. "Very truly, I tell you, if you ask anything of the Father in my name, he will give it to you" (John 16:23). In fact, far from waiting for us to find him, Jesus indicates that he has already sought us out and is waiting for us to respond. "Listen! I am standing at the door, knocking; if you hear my voice and open the door, I will come in to you and eat with you, and you with me" (Rev. 3:20). We do not have to create or earn this relationship. It is all about receiving and being grateful to the One who has called us.

Jesus also taught that after he had risen from the dead and returned to heaven, he would send the Holy Spirit to empower believers to do his work in the world. The Holy Spirit is the living presence of Jesus in our world today. The Spirit also is ours for the asking. Again Jesus promises that God will give us what we need to be faithful when he says, "If you then, who are evil, know how to give good gifts to your children, how much more will the heavenly Father give the Holy Spirit to those who ask" (Luke 11:13).

Spiritual leaders are always dependent on the God who calls them. We cannot bear any fruit independently. Jesus speaks stern words to those who would try to go it alone: "Whoever does not abide in me is thrown away like a branch and withers; such branches are gathered, thrown into the fire, and burned" (John 15:6). Our own efforts, no matter how tireless and selfless, cannot produce the results that God wants to see. Rather, the fruit we are called to bear will come as we reach out to receive the power and provision from Christ through the Holy Spirit.

3. *Gather the manna daily.* Exodus 16 tells the story of how God provided for the needs of the children of Israel while they were traveling through the desert. God sent a fine, flaky substance upon the ground, and the people were told to gather it, cook it, and eat it. This was their

"bread" and would strengthen them for the journey. An interesting detail in this story is that the Israelites were told to gather only just as much as they needed for the day, and not to keep extra manna overnight. Some of the people kept it anyway and found that it went bad by the next day.

God still provides what we need to be God's faithful people and to serve God. God has provided all kinds of resources for us, including worship, prayer, Bible study and meditation, meeting together in groups for support, conferences, classes, and sacraments. Spiritual nourishment is available to us every day. Our responsibility is to gather the manna for our spiritual support day by day. It would be nice if we could gather it every now and then and live on that experience without making the daily effort. However, this plan is about as practical as someone who decides only to eat physical food once a month or once a year. The glow of the church conference you attended or the message of the wonderful book you read last month will soon lose its power and become a vague memory. The daily walk and communion with God will change your life and give you the resources to be faithful.

The best practice is to find your most effective way to gather the manna, and then to do it as often as possible, at least several times a week. This is where personality and temperament come into play. Some people love quiet time and are delighted with any excuse to go into solitude and commune with God. Others, however, feel God's presence best with other people, in corporate worship or in small groups or one-on-one. Some connect with God through study and reflection; others get there through actively and mindfully doing things for Jesus' sake. Still others are fed when they look at art or listen to music. Then there are people who feel God's presence most clearly when they are out in nature. The important thing is to find your way and practice it often.

Unfortunately the majority of the books about spiritual nurture have been written by people who meet God best in silence and solitude. Reading these books tends to make people who experience God in other ways feel that they have somehow missed the mark. However, there is no one right way to seek God. The best practice is to find your best and most effective way to be in communion with God and practice it as often as possible. If you are a morning person, do it in the morning. If you are an evening person, do it before you go to bed. Ancient traditions of the church suggest that putting the day in God's hands at the beginning, then examining the day in God's forgiving, redeeming presence at night will bear much fruit. But whenever and however you do it, seek this close communion—this vine-and-branch abiding—as close to daily as possible.

I imagine that for the early Israelites, manna gathering was a communal enterprise, with groups of people doing it together and enjoying each other's company in the process. Throughout Christian history believers have sought God's presence and encouragement for the journey of faith in small groups. Such groups create a safe space where people can be honest about themselves. In small groups we are heard by others and given the chance to listen to how other people experience God. We can share the struggle of others in small groups, confident that what is shared stays in the group. If you are interested in serious manna gathering, it might be helpful to find a group of like-minded people to seek spiritual growth with you over a period of time.

A variation on this theme is for officers who want to grow in the faith to find a mentor. This approach can be especially helpful for new elders and deacons. Find another layperson who models effective spiritual leadership, and learn everything you can. Draw on the mentor as a resource when you face difficult challenges. Ask questions and seek her or his wisdom. Be confident and vent frustrations and complaints that should not be taken home to the family. Elders who have served many terms and retired from active service make particularly good mentors. Along with a wise adviser, a prayer partner is also a very helpful way of finding support as you seek to be a spiritual leader. This partner could be any person of prayer with whom you feel comfortable sharing your concerns and needs, knowing that they will be kept in confidence.

4. *Share the work.* One of the things that has undone many a church officer is the inability to delegate. Some people find it hard to ask others to do things because they don't want to impose. Others fear being told no. Others simply find it too much trouble. Instead of taking the time to make the contacts, they would rather do it themselves. However, effective spiritual leaders know that what one person can accomplish is never as much as a motivated group of people can do. Reluctance to share the work limits what can be done for God in your particular area of responsibility. Often people want to be involved and are only waiting to be asked. Inviting them to participate is a way of sharing the joy of serving Christ. Inviting new members to participate is also a way to fold them into the life of the church, help them get to know people and do something meaningful, and keep them from drifting away.

Some officers find themselves doing all the work themselves because time runs out and they have not done the advance work required to ask others to help. Taking time to plan and distribute the work in committee meetings can keep you out of this situation. Recurring tasks such as preparing Communion elements can be delegated by setting up a yearly schedule and getting people to sign up in advance. As the year goes along, all the leader needs to do is call and remind people of their commitment. Don't be shy about asking a veteran elder or deacon to help you learn how to delegate. Learning this skill may be challenging, but it may save you from burnout and also enable you to share the joy of doing significant things for God with many people.

5. *Set appropriate boundaries.* Operating in the freedom Christ gives to us enables church officers to set three very important boundaries. One is being able to say no. Not everything that you are asked to do is appropriate for you to do. Not everything that needs doing is your God-given call. Wearing the yoke of Christ and having a sense of what he has called you to do enable you to discern when to say no and when to say yes. It is as wrong to say yes inappropriately as it is to say no inappropriately. Saying yes to everything that comes your way leads to overfunctioning and is a sure road to exhaustion.

A second important boundary involves knowing when something is your problem and when it is not. The section on triangling in chapter 8 treats this issue in more detail. Suffice it to say that many officers waste significant amounts of energy getting involved in matters that are really none of their business. In so doing they waste valuable emotional capital and may even make the situations worse. Part of effective self-care is learning to put problems where they can best be addressed and to stay out of the middle of the conflicts of others. For instance, if you are on the education committee and someone comes to you to complain about the church's landscaping, gently suggest that they need to talk to the property committee instead and tell them who is the chair of that committee. When someone comes to you complaining about another person, urge her or him to sort out those issues with that person face to face. This approach to such difficulties sets wholesome boundaries and is much healthier for the church in the long run.

A third important boundary is to protect worship and nurture time at church. I have heard a number of officers say they have grown weary of going to church because people will not leave them alone to worship or study. It is just too easy for members of the congregation to unload on officers in Sunday school, circle meeting, or during the worship hour. Staff members who attend worship where they work are also vulnerable to this problem. Church can become a to-do list, and the joy of communion with God and others can be lost. Prudent officers will discern when they need to be allowed simply to be a member of the congregation, and they will protect those times. One clerk of session I knew when approached in the sanctuary by a church member with an addition to the to-do list would reply, "Could you please call me about that this afternoon when we have more time to talk?" He was setting a healthy boundary while at the same time showing concern to the person in need.

Spiritual leaders are not called to carry the church on their shoulders. You are not called to save the world; Jesus already did this. You are simply called to be as faithful as you can to the tasks God has placed before you. This in itself is usually challenging enough. To those flirting with burnout, hear Jesus say, "Come to me, all you that are weary and are carrying heavy burdens, and I will give you rest. Take my yoke upon you, and learn from me; for I am gentle and humble in heart, and you will find rest for your souls" (Matt. 11:28–29). All servants of the Christ are invited here to turn away from soul-crushing loads of responsibility and to focus attention on Jesus, on his presence, his call, his resources. When we do this, our strength is renewed, and we bear good fruit.

QUESTIONS FOR THOUGHT AND DISCUSSION

1. If you have served as a church officer before, has your experience been more like that of Tim or of Dawn in the vignette at the beginning of this chapter? What could have been done to help you be more effective?
2. How could the way your congregation's officer nominating committee does its work be changed to help new officers get off to a better start?
3. What can pastors do to enhance the authority of elders and deacons as spiritual leaders?
4. How does your congregation show appreciation to its officers? Do the officers feel appreciated and valued for their work?
5. Have you ever experienced having your worship or education time at church interrupted by people who want to talk church business with you? If so, how do you handle it?
6. Where in your life do you find quality time with God? How does this time help you in your spiritual leadership?

Notes

Chapter One

1. Emil Brunner, "The Christian Doctrine of the Church, Faith, and the Consummation," in *Dogmatics,* trans. David Cairns (Philadelphia: Westminster Press, 1960), 3:6.
2. R. Alastair Campbell, *The Elders* (Edinburgh, U.K.: Baker, 1994), 150.
3. David W. Bennett, *Metaphors for Ministry: Biblical Images for Leaders and Followers* (Carlisle, U.K.: Paternoster Press, 1993), 150.
4. Ibid., 151.
5. Paul S. Wright, *The Duties of the Ruling Elder* (Philadelphia: Westminster Press, 1957), 24–25.
6. John Calvin, *Institutes of the Christian Religion,* ed. John T. McNeill, trans. Ford Lewis Battles, LCC (Philadelphia: Westminster Press, 1960), 4.3.9.
7. James B. Ramsey, *The Deaconship* (Richmond, VA: Presbyterian Publishing Committee, 1879), 17, 26–27.

Chapter Two

1. Lyle E. Schaller, "What Are the Sources of Authority?" in *The Parish Papers,* 20, no. 5 (January 1991): 1.
2. This discussion of types of authority and how they are achieved draws on Schaller's article cited above.

Chapter Five

1. See Marva J. Dawn, *Reaching Out without Dumbing Down: A Theology of Worship for the Turn-of-the-Century Church* (Grand Rapids: Eerdmans, 1995).
2. *The Constitution of the Presbyterian Church (U.S.A.),* Part I, *Book of Confessions* (Louisville, KY: Office of the General Assembly, Presbyterian Church (U.S.A.), 1999), 6.002.
3. Ibid., 7.003A.
4. Ibid., 3.18.
5. Calvin, *Institutes,* 1.9.3.
6. Alan Richardson, ed., *A Theological Wordbook of the Bible* (New York: Macmillan, 1971), 258.

Chapter Six

1. This section draws from the following: Norman Shawchuck, *Taking a Look at Your Leadership Styles* (Downers Grove, IL: Organizational Resources Press, 1980); W. Engstrom and Edward R. Drayton, *The Art of Management for Christian Leaders* (Grand Rapids: Zondervan, 1989); and Lyle E. Schaller, *Getting Things Done* (Nashville: Abingdon, 1986).

2. Schaller, *Getting Things Done*, 178.

3. James E. Means, *Leadership in Christian Ministry* (Grand Rapids: Baker Book House, 1989), 82.

4. Ibid., 86–87.

5. Shawchuck, *Taking a Look at Your Leadership Styles*, 20.

Chapter Seven

1. *Book of Confessions*, 1.2.

2. Shirley C. Guthrie Jr., *Christian Doctrine* (Richmond, VA: CLC Press, 1968), 355.

3. Ibid., 360.

Chapter Eight

1. Edwin H. Friedman, *Generation to Generation: Family Process in Church and Synagogue* (New York: Guilford Press, 1985), 1.

2. Ronald Richardson, *Creating a Healthier Church* (Minneapolis: Fortress Press, 1996), 133–37. I have drawn extensively on this book and also on Peter Steinke, *How Your Church Family Works* (Washington, DC: Alban Institute, 1993), in my discussion of family systems theory in this chapter.

3. Friedman, *Generation to Generation*, 212.

4. Richardson, *Creating a Healthier Church*, 50–51, 173.

5. Friedman, *Generation to Generation*, 229.

Chapter Nine

1. *Book of Confessions*, 7.113A.

2. Presbyterian Church (U.S.A.), *The Presbyterian Hymnal* (Louisville, KY: Westminster/John Knox Press, 1990), 260.

Resources for Further Study

For those wishing to know more about discernment:

Danny E. Morris and Charles M. Olsen, *Discerning God's Will Together* (Nashville: Upper Room Books, 1997).

Elizabeth Liebert, *The Way of Discernment: Spiritual Practices for Decision Making* (Louisville, KY: Westminster John Knox Press, 2008).

For those wishing to know more about spiritual disciplines:

Daniel Wolpert, *Creating a Life with God* (Nashville: Upper Room Books, 2003).

Daniel Wolpert, *Leading a Life with God* (Nashville: Upper Room Books, 2006).

Marjorie Thompson, *Soul Feast* (Louisville, KY: Westminster John Knox Press, 1995).

For those wishing to know how to revitalize session meetings:

Charles M. Olsen, *Transforming Church Boards into Communities of Spiritual Leaders* (Washington, DC: Alban Institute Publications, 1995).

Index

CPSIA information can be obtained
at www.ICGtesting.com
Printed in the USA
FSHW02n0752290518
48802FS

9 780664 503055